PREPARING FOR THE SHRM-CP® EXAM

Workbook and 70 Practice Questions from SHRM

Second Edition

PREPARING FOR THE SHRM-CP® EXAM

WORKBOOK AND 70 PRACTICE QUESTIONS FROM SHRM

SECOND EDITION

Editors: Charles Glover, MS Manager, Exam Development & Accreditation, SHRM and Nancy A. Woolever, MAIS, SHRM-SCP, Vice President, Academic, Certification, and Student Communities

Copyright © 2025 SHRM. All rights reserved.

This publication is designed to provide accurate and authoritative information regarding the subject matter covered. It is sold with the understanding that neither the publisher nor the author is engaged in rendering legal or other professional service. If legal advice or other expert assistance is required, the services of a competent, licensed professional should be sought. The federal and state laws discussed in this book are subject to frequent revision and interpretation by amendments or judicial revisions that may significantly affect employer or employee rights and obligations. Readers are encouraged to seek legal counsel regarding specific policies and practices in their organizations.

This book is published by SHRM, the Society for Human Resource Management. The interpretations, conclusions, and recommendations in this book are those of the author and do not necessarily represent those of the publisher.

This publication may not be reproduced, stored in a retrieval system, or transmitted in whole or in part, in any form or by any means, electronic, mechanical, photocopying, recording, or otherwise, without the prior written permission of the publisher, or authorization through payment of the appropriate per-copy fee to the Copyright Clearance Center, Inc., 222 Rosewood Drive, Danvers, MA 01923, 978-750-8600, fax 978-646-8600, or on the Web at www.copyright.com. Requests to the publisher for permission should be addressed to SHRM Book Permissions, 1800 Duke Street, Alexandria, VA 22314, or online at http://www.shrm.org/about-shrm/pages/copyright--permissions.aspx. SHRM books and products are available on most online bookstores and through the SHRMStore at www.shrmstore.org.

SHRM is a member-driven catalyst for creating better workplaces where people and businesses thrive together. As the trusted authority on all things work, SHRM is the foremost expert, researcher, advocate, and thought leader on issues and innovations impacting today's evolving workplaces. With nearly 340,000 members in 180 countries, SHRM touches the lives of more than 362 million workers and their families globally. Discover more at SHRM.org.

ISBN 9781586447151 (paperback)
ISBN 9781586447205 (pdf)
ISBN 9781586447250 (epub)
ISBN 9781586447274 (kindle)

All product names, logos, and brands are property of their respective owners in the United States and/or other countries. All company, product and service names used on this website are for identification purposes only.

SHRM®, SHRM-CP®, SHRM-SCP®, Learning System®, SHRM BASK™, and the "SHRM" logo are registered trademarks of SHRM.

Published in the United States of America

SECOND EDITION   2025 REVISED PRINTING

PB Printing   10 9 8 7 6 5 4 3 2

Contents

Acknowledgments

This workbook was made possible by the thoughtful and generous advice, guidance, and input of many smart and talented subject matter experts, especially the following:

Mike Aitken, executive vice president, HR Professional Solutions, SHRM

Alexander Alonso, PhD, SHRM-SCP, chief data & insights officer, SHRM

Nicholas Schacht, SHRM-SCP, chief commercial officer, SHRM

Jeanne Morris, senior vice president, Consumer Products, SHRM

Patricia Byrd, SHRM-SCP, director, Credentialing Services, SHRM

Susie Davis, director, Education Products, SHRM

Hanna Evans, SHRM-CP, senior specialist, Form Development, SHRM

Eddice L. Douglas, SHRM-CP, lead, Educational Products, SHRM

Sarah Chuon, SHRM-CP, specialist, Exam Development, SHRM

Giselle Calliste, SHRM-CP, specialist, Exam HR Content, SHRM

Morgan Fecto, Exam Development, SHRM

Scott Oppler, PhD, senior technical advisor, Human Resource Research Organization (HumRRO)

Laura Steighner, PhD, president, Steighner Solutions

Kelly Cusick, senior vice president, Marketing, Holmes Corporation

Caitlin Shea, SHRM-CP, product manager, Holmes Corporation

We also gratefully acknowledge the scores of SHRM members, SHRM certificate holders, and exam candidates who provided input for this book.

Introduction

We applaud your decision to move your career in Human Resources forward by pursuing a certification with SHRM! To this end, this workbook is designed to help you prepare for the **SHRM Certified Professional (SHRM-CP©)** exam.

Specifically, the SHRM-CP exam is designed to determine who has the level of competency and knowledge that is expected for HR professionals who perform (or will perform) operational work. This includes such duties as implementing policies, serving as the HR point of contact, performing day-to-day HR functions, and much more.

In this second edition, we have placed a greater emphasis on utilizing and understanding the SHRM Body of Applied Skills and Knowledge (SHRM BASK®)—bridging the knowledge, concepts, and competencies that the SHRM BASK encapsulates to the SHRM-CP exams. Perhaps most importantly, this workbook includes a total of 70 practice items that were used on past SHRM-CP exams. These practice items will provide you with more exposure to the types of items that you will see on the real exam, as well as feedback about correct responses. These items were not simply created for this book—they were taken from actual SHRM-CP exams that were used in previous years.

On the other hand, the SHRM Senior Certified Professional (SHRM-SCP) designation is for HR professionals who are advanced in their careers. This level of professional primarily works in a strategic role, such as developing policies and strategies, overseeing the execution of integrated HR operations, directing the entire HR enterprise, and leading the alignment of HR strategies to organizational goals. Although the SHRM-CP and SHRM-SCP exams are very similar in structure, this workbook is focused exclusively on the SHRM-CP exam.

It is important to note that this workbook is designed to be used along with the official SHRM study guide: *Ace Your SHRM Certification Exam: The Official SHRM Study Guide for the SHRM-CP and SHRM-SCP Exams,* the SHRM BASK, and the SHRM Learning System®. The study guide includes much additional information about the exam and exam preparation strategies, and it also includes a set of practice items from a combination of the SHRM-CP and SHRM-SCP exams. The SHRM BASK reflects the blueprint for the SHRM-CP exam and should be used to develop your study plan. The SHRM Learning System is the comprehensive preparation tool offered by SHRM built upon the SHRM BASK.

In this SHRM-CP workbook, some of the key concepts that were introduced in the study guide are further explained. For example, a self-assessment for gauging strengths and development areas that are addressed in the exam was briefly introduced in the study guide; this is created in the current workbook to help with SHRM-CP exam preparation.

Thank you for allowing SHRM to embark on this journey with you toward SHRM-CP certification and beyond!

How to Apply

SHRM offers both certification exams during two testing windows every year. The first window is from May 1 to July 15, and the second window is from December 1 to February 15. Examinees can choose to take the exam in person at one of more than 500 Prometric testing centers across more than 180 countries, or you can choose to take it via live remote proctoring.

Once you have decided which exam to take, register to take the exam on the SHRM website anytime between the Applications Accepted Starting Date and the Standard Application Deadline.

Examinees who apply by the **Early-Bird Application Deadline** and/or who are **SHRM members** receive a reduced exam fee. Note that exam applications apply to specific testing windows; once you have applied, transferring to the next testing window is possible for an additional fee.

To learn more about the benefits of SHRM memberships, receive discounts on the SHRM Learning System and the SHRM Certification exams, and much more, navigate to this link: https://www.shrm.org/membership.

To apply, you must

1. Apply online (https://www.shrm.org/credentials/certification),

2. Create a user account,

3. Select the exam level you want to take,

4. Complete the application form and sign the SHRM Certification Candidate Agreement,

5. Pay the application fee, and

6. Once you receive your Authorization-to-Test (ATT) letter, schedule your exam directly through SHRM's test delivery vendor (https://www.prometric.com/shrm). Your ATT letter will outline several ways to schedule your exam and select your testing location/modality (test in person or via remote proctoring).

SHRM-CP and SHRM-SCP Eligibility

SHRM Certified Professional (SHRM-CP)

- The SHRM-CP certification is intended for individuals who perform general HR or HR-related duties, or for currently enrolled students and individuals pursuing a career in Human Resource Management.
- Candidates for the SHRM-CP certification are not required to hold an HR title and do not need a degree or previous HR experience to apply; however, a basic working knowledge of HR practices and principles or a degree from an Academically Aligned program is recommended.
- The SHRM-CP exam is designed to assess the competency level of HR at the operational level. This level includes implementing policies, supporting day-to-day HR functions, or serving as an HR point of contact for staff and stakeholders.
- Refer to the SHRM BASK for detailed information on proficiency standards for this credential (i.e., Proficiency Indicators only for All HR Professionals).

SHRM Senior Certified Professional (SHRM-SCP)

- The SHRM-SCP certification is for individuals who have a work history of at least **three years performing strategic level HR or HR-related duties,** or for SHRM-CP credential holders who have held the credential for at least three years and are working in, or are in the process of transitioning to, a strategic level role.
- Candidates for the SHRM-SCP certification are not required to hold an HR title and do not need a degree to apply.
- The SHRM-SCP exam is designed to assess the competency level of those who engage in HR work at the strategic level. Work at this level includes duties such as developing HR policies and/or procedures, overseeing the execution of integrated HR operations, directing an entire HR enterprise, or leading the alignment of HR strategies to organizational goals.
- Applicants must be able to demonstrate that they devoted at least 1,000 hours per calendar year (Jan.–Dec.) to strategic-level HR or HR-related work.
  - More than 1,000 hours in a calendar year does not equate to more than one year of experience.
  - Part-time work qualifies as long as the 1,000-hour per calendar year standard is met.
  - Experience may be either salaried or hourly.
- Individuals who are HR consultants may demonstrate qualifying experience through the HR or HR-related duties they perform for their clients. Contracted hours must meet the 1,000-hour standard.
- Refer to the SHRM BASK for detailed information on proficiency standards for this credential (i.e., Proficiency Indicators for All HR Professionals and for Advanced HR Professionals).

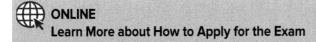

ONLINE
Learn More about How to Apply for the Exam

https://www.shrm.org/credentials/certification/how-to-get-shrm-certified-process

Testing Options

Why Might Remote-Proctored Testing Be a Good Option for Me?

There are many reasons people choose to test remotely. One of these reasons might fit your circumstances:

» Testing in a familiar place helps put you at ease.

» The nearest test center is farther away than you wish to travel.

» The convenience of testing anytime and anywhere gives you more control over your experience.

» There are no in-person seats available at the time you want to test.

Why Might Remote-Proctored Testing NOT Be a Good Option for Me?

Remote-proctored testing isn't for everyone. When you take a SHRM certification exam via remote proctoring, your home or office *becomes* the testing center. This means you are responsible for ensuring the security of your exam as well as providing the computer and internet connection to complete the exam. Here are some strong reasons why remote proctoring might *not* be the best option for you:

» You do not have access to a computer that meets Prometric's system requirements.

» You do not have a strong, stable internet connection.

» You do not have a quiet, private room (with a door that closes) at your home or office to take the exam.

» You want to have immediate access to an in-person test center administrator in case something goes wrong with your exam.

To ensure you are making an informed decision, check out this link to decide if remote proctoring or in-person testing is right for you: https://www.prometric.com/proproctorcandidate.

Section 1

The SHRM-CP Exam Structure

Types of Exam Items

As defined in the *Ace Your SHRM Certification Exam* study guide and on the SHRM website, there are two general types of items on the SHRM-CP exam: (1) knowledge items (KIs) and foundational knowledge items (FKIs); and (2) situational judgment items (SJIs).

Knowledge items (including FKIs) are stand-alone multiple-choice items with four response options. Each KI tests a single piece of knowledge or application of knowledge.

Situational judgment items (SJIs) present realistic situations from workplaces throughout the world. Based on the scenario presented, SJIs ask test takers to consider the problem presented in the question within the context of the situation, and then select the best course of action to take. As with the KIs, these are multiple-choice items with four response options.

The distribution of items with respect to content and item type is essentially the same for both the SHRM-CP and SHRM-SCP exams. About half of the items on each exam are allocated across the three behavioral competency clusters, and the other half are allocated across the three HR knowledge domains. Approximately 40% of the items on each exam are situational judgment items, and the remainder are stand-alone items measuring either knowledge that is foundational to the behavioral competencies (10%) or HR-specific knowledge (50%).

Item Type

Situational Judgment (40%)	HR-Specific Knowledge (50%)
Foundational Knowledge (10%)	

Behavioral Competency Clusters

Leadership (17%)

Business (16.5%)

Interpersonal (16.5%)

HR Knowledge Domains

People (18%)

Organization (18%)

Workplace (14%)

Exam Items

The SHRM-CP exam consists of a total of 134 questions—110 of the questions are scored, and 24 of the questions are unscored. The purpose of unscored items is to gather data to determine if they are viable to become scored test items on future SHRM exams if they perform well. Think of unscored items like beta testing to gather tester data. While unscored items will not affect your overall score (getting unscored items incorrect will not count against you), it is important not to skip any questions.

The scored and unscored items are intermingled throughout the exam and are indiscernible from one another. This exam is broken into two equal halves, and each half contains 67 questions.

Each half is divided into three sections:

» **Section 1:** 20 KIs and FKIs (i.e., knowledge items for behavioral competencies)

» **Section 2:** 27 SJIs

» **Section 3:** 20 KIs and FKIs

Exam Timing

The total exam appointment time is four hours, which includes **three hours and forty minutes** of testing time for the exam itself. This equals approximately 90 seconds per question. It is important to use your time wisely.

It is critical to note that you will be unable to return to Exam Half 1 upon moving to Exam Half 2. Ensure that you have answered all of the questions to the best of your ability in Exam Half 1 before proceeding to the second half of the exam. There will be confirmatory prompts for you before transitioning to Exam Half 2.

The exam time is broken down into the following segments:

» **Introduction,** including confidentiality reminder: four minutes

» **Tutorial:** eight minutes

» **Exam Half 1:** up to one hour and fifty minutes

» **Exam Half 2:** up to one hour and fifty minutes

» **Post Exam Survey:** six minutes

There are a few transition screens throughout the exam that account for the remaining minutes.

Section 2

Understanding the SHRM BASK

One of the most important things for you to understand as you prepare for the SHRM-CP exam is this:

All of the HR competencies and knowledge areas that are assessed on the SHRM-CP exam are detailed in the SHRM BASK.

Conceptually, preparing for the SHRM-CP exam is not unlike preparing for the SHRM-SCP exam. Do not be fooled, however—they are completely different exams by design, emphasizing differences found in the **proficiency indicators** area of the SHRM BASK. Before deciding whether or not the SHRM-CP exam is right for you, it is critical to match your knowledge and experience with the key concepts and proficiency indicators with those in the SHRM BASK for **All HR Professionals** ensuring you feel comfortable and confident with the material.

While the SHRM-CP and SHRM-SCP share the same blueprint, the exams are designed to be completely distinct by way of using proficiency indicators to separate the knowledge, skills, and abilities required to address *operational-level* (SHRM-CP) HR duties and tasks versus *strategic-level* (SHRM-SCP) HR functions and responsibilities.

The SHRM BASK can also be thought of as the blueprint for the SHRM-CP exam, much like an architect uses a blueprint to construct a building, testing programs use an 'exam blueprint' to build examinations. You can find the complete version of the SHRM BASK at:

https://www.shrm.org/credentials/certification/exam-preparation/body-of-applied-skills-and-knowledge

Important reminders as you prepare for the SHRM-CP exam:

» If something is not covered in the SHRM BASK, it is not eligible for the SHRM-CP exam. However, the SHRM BASK is an expansive document that covers many different areas, and given its breadth, you might not see everything that is presented in the SHRM BASK represented on the SHRM-CP exam in any given testing window.

» The SHRM BASK does not define your specific HR role, but rather the HR professional role in general. Therefore, it may cover more than your current or past HR roles.

» For individuals testing outside of the U.S., you are not held accountable for content covered in the U.S. Employment Law & Regulations section of the SHRM BASK (Workplace content domain). Those items will be substituted with items from the Workplace domain.

This workbook is designed to demystify the SHRM BASK, providing insights to aid your test preparation using the SHRM BASK as a study tool. In this section, we provide guidance on how to

Figure 2.1. The SHRM BASK Model

break the SHRM BASK into digestible segments to help you identify areas of strength and areas that you need to study more, ultimately creating a personalized study guide in preparation for the SHRM-CP exam.

Structure of the SHRM BASK

Simply reading through the SHRM BASK may be a daunting task due to the amount of information it contains. Before tackling the detail, it can be helpful to understand the structure and the elements comprising the model. Let's start with the basics.

» HR technical competency; divided into three content domains: *People*, *Organization*, and *Workplace*.

» Behavioral competency; divided into three content clusters: *Business*, *Interpersonal*, and *Leadership*.

The HR technical competency, **HR Expertise**, reflects the technical knowledge specific to the HR field for an HR professional to perform their role. **Behavioral competencies**, on the other hand, describe the knowledge, skills, abilities and other characteristics (KSAOs) that define proficient performance for a professional. They are more general in their applicability than the profession-specific technical competency. That is, many of these competencies may apply to different jobs, roles and professions but have been specifically defined in HR terms for the SHRM BASK.

In short, the HR Expertise technical competencies reflect what knowledge HR professionals apply on the job, and behavioral competencies reflect how they apply this knowledge.

Before we dig deeper, Figure 2.2 presents a high-level overview of the SHRM BASK structure including how Key Concepts (KC) or Proficiency Indicators (PI), or both, support the content area you are studying. Ensure you review the applicable Key Concepts and Proficiency Indicators, where applicable.

HR Expertise		
People	**Organization**	**Workplace**
» HR Strategy KC/PI » Talent Acquisition KC/PI » Employee Engagement & Retention KC/PI » Learning & Development KC/PI » Total Rewards KC/PI	» Structure of the HR Function KC/PI » Organizational Effectiveness & Development KC/PI » Workforce Management KC/PI » Employee & Labor Relations KC/PI » Technology Management KC/PI	» Managing a Global Workforce KC/PI » Risk Management KC/PI » Corporate Social Responsibility KC/PI » *U.S. Employment Law & Regulations KC/PI

Behavioral Competencies			
Leadership	**Leadership & Navigation** KC	**Ethical Practice** KC	**Inclusion & Diversity** KC
	» Navigating the Organization PI » Vision PI » Managing HR Initiatives PI » Influence PI	» Personal Integrity PI » Professional Integrity PI » Ethical Agent PI	» Creating an Inclusive and Diverse Culture PI » Ensuring Equity Effectiveness PI » Connecting I&D to Organizational Performance PI
Interpersonal	**Relationship Management** KC	**Communication** KC	**Global Mindset** KC
	» Networking PI » Relationship Building PI » Teamwork PI » Negotiation PI » Conflict Management PI	» Delivering Messages PI » Exchanging Organizational Information PI » Listening PI	» Operating in a Culturally Diverse Workplace PI » Operating in a Global Environment PI » Advocating for a Culturally Inclusive and Diverse Workplace PI
Business	**Business Acumen** KC	**Consultation** KC	**Analytical Aptitude** KC
	» Business and Competitive Awareness PI » Business Analysis PI » Strategic Alignment PI	» Evaluating Business Challenges PI » Designing HR Solutions PI » Advising on HR Solutions PI » Change Management PI » Service Excellence PI	» Data Advocate PI » Data Gathering PI » Data Analysis PI » Evidence-Based Decision-Making PI

*U.S. Employment Law & Regulations content will only appear if you are testing within the U.S. If you are testing elsewhere across the globe, via in-person testing or report proctoring, those items will be substituted with other items from the Workplace HR Expertise domain.

Figure 2.2. Overall Structure of the SHRM BASK

HR Expertise

The HR technical competency, HR Expertise, reflects the principles, practices, and functions of effective HR management. This competency is grouped into three main knowledge domains: **People, Organization, and Workplace**. The knowledge domains are further divided into 14 HR functional knowledge areas that describe the technical knowledge required to perform key HR activities.

» **People:** HR Strategy, Talent Acquisition, Employee Engagement & Retention, Learning & Development, and Total Rewards

» **Organization:** Structure of the HR Function, Organizational Effectiveness & Development, Workforce Management, Employee & Labor Relations, and Technology Management

» **Workplace:** Managing a Global Workforce, Risk Management, Corporate Social Responsibility, and U.S. Law & Regulations

Each HR technical competency includes the following information:

» Definition of the functional area,

» Key concepts describing the knowledge specific to the functional area, and

» Proficiency indicators that apply to **All HR Professionals** (i.e., early career through executive career levels) as well as those that apply primarily to **Advanced HR Professionals** (i.e., senior and executive career levels).

  › Note that for the SHRM-CP, proficiency indicators for All HR Professionals are the key ones to attend to.

Behavioral Competencies

Behavioral competencies facilitate the application of technical knowledge. Successful HR professionals must understand and effectively perform the behavioral components of HR practice in addition to being in command of technical HR knowledge. The nine behavioral competencies are grouped into three clusters:

» **Business**: Business Acumen, Consultation, and Analytical Aptitude

» **Interpersonal**: Relationship Management, Communication, and Global Mindset

» **Leadership**: Leadership & Navigation, Ethical Practice, and Inclusion & Diversity

Unlike the HR technical competency, each behavioral competency is further comprised of three to five sub-competencies for a total of thirty-three sub-competencies. Refer back to Figure 2.2 for an overview of the sub-competencies by their competency and cluster. For each behavioral competency, the following information is provided:

» Definition of the competency,

» Key concepts describing the foundational knowledge for the competency,

» Sub-competencies applicable to the competency, with definitions, and

» Proficiency indicators that apply to all HR professionals as well as those that apply primarily to advanced HR professionals.

> Similarly, proficiency indicators for all HR professionals are the key ones to attend to when preparing for the SHRM-CP exam.

Key Concepts and Proficiency Indicators

Structural Difference in the SHRM BASK

In addition to the what and how distinction between HR Expertise and behavioral competencies, another difference important to understanding the structure of the SHRM BASK focuses on where the key concepts and proficiency indicators are specified in the model.

As depicted in Figure 2.2, key concepts (KC) and proficiency indicators (PI) are specified for each knowledge area under **HR Expertise** technical competency (note the superscripts beside each knowledge area). However, behavioral competencies are structured differently in this regard: Key concepts are identified by behavioral competency, and proficiency indicators are identified by sub-competency.

The SHRM-CP certification focuses on the proficiency indicators identified for *All HR Professionals*, and the SHRM-SCP certification exam focuses only on the indicators identified for *Advanced HR Professionals*. Although the proficiency indicators relevant to all HR professionals clearly apply to advanced HR professionals at the senior and executive levels, they are not assessed directly on these indicators but are expected, on the job, to understand the concepts behind these functions, recognize their strategic importance, and be able to mentor junior employees in developing those behaviors.

Example of Parallel Proficiency Indicators

An example of this distinction can be seen by parallel proficiency indicators presented under the *Corporate Social Responsibility* (CSR) knowledge area within the Workplace functional knowledge domain.

» For **Advanced HR Professionals**: *Develops a CSR strategy that reflects the organization's mission and values.*

» For **All HR Professionals**: *Identifies and promotes opportunities for HR and the organization to engage in CSR activities that align with the organization's CSR strategy.*

Both proficiency indicators address the organization's CSR strategy. The *advanced* proficiency indicator highlights the higher-level organizational focus of developing this strategy, whereas the *all* proficiency indicator focuses on supporting the strategy by identifying and promoting opportunities in alignment with the organizational strategy.

How to Use the SHRM BASK for Studying

Now that you have an understanding of the overall structure of the SHRM BASK, the next step is to understand the format of exam items and how you can leverage the information in the SHRM BASK to help your preparation for the exam.

Item Types

Both the SHRM-CP and SHRM-SCP certification exams consist of two types of items: knowledge items (KIs)[1] and situational judgment items (SJIs).

Knowledge Items

KIs are stand-alone, multiple-choice items that test a single piece of knowledge or application of knowledge and make up 60% of the exam. Topics stem from the key concepts and proficiency indicators presented throughout the SHRM BASK.

Each KI assesses content knowledge according to one of four possible cognitive classifications, or levels of understanding or application, required to answer it:

» **Recall** items test the facts for that key concept such as defining a specific term or identifying a component of a theoretical model. This is the most basic type of KI.

» **Understanding** items requires the test taker to demonstrate their content knowledge by comprehending information, comparing two things, translating by applying knowledge or interpreting a concept to apply it to an example. These items assess the test taker's ability to recognize how HR concepts and terms manifest themselves in the workplace.

» **Problem-solving** items require test takers to apply their knowledge to develop a solution to a problem, which is something HR professionals do every day. To select the correct answer, the test taker must draw on their knowledge and understanding of many different concepts and strategies, which is more cognitively demanding than simply recalling the information.

» **Critical evaluation** items ask test takers to analyze information to predict an outcome. A competent HR professional uses the ability to predict outcomes to guide business strategy and execution.

Situational Judgement Items

In comparison, SJIs test decision-making and judgment skills to identify the most effective response according to HR best practices, as established by HR subject matter experts. These items make up 40% of the exam, and involve three major components:

» A realistic situation (scenario) that is similar to what many HR professionals have likely experienced during their careers,

---

1.   The Ace Your SHRM Certification Exam: *The Official SHRM Study Guide for the SHRM-CP and SHRM-SCP Exams* references two types of knowledge items: KIs and foundational KIs (FKIs). KIs and FKIs follow the same structure; the only meaningful difference is that the content for a KI stem from a knowledge area under *HR Expertise*, whereas the content for an FKI stem from a *behavioral competency*. For this workbook, we refer to all knowledge items as KIs.

» Two to three questions addressing the scenario prompting test takers to solve a particular situation-specific issue in an action-oriented way, and

» Four possible response options.

For example, while a KI may test your knowledge about different communication elements or techniques (for example, under the *Communication* behavioral competency), an SJI may ask you to identify the most effective way to communicate with leaders or with the organization given the circumstances presented in the scenario. In lieu of being able to assess each test taker's real-life response to the same situation, an SJI offers an opportunity for test takers to leverage their knowledge of key concepts, as well as HR best practices, to demonstrate how they might have responded to a similar real-life situation.

For more information about these item types, please refer to the SHRM Learning System or *Ace Your SHRM Certification Exam.*

Creating a Study Guide from the SHRM BASK

As noted previously, simply reading the SHRM BASK may be overwhelming and, as a result, not particularly helpful as a test preparation approach. Rather, the model needs to be consumed in smaller bites. In the remainder of this section, we present an approach to examining the different components of the SHRM BASK to identify particular topics to study and further investigate during your test preparation.

First, we recommend picking a knowledge area or behavioral competency and sub-competency as a starting point. From there, you will leverage the key concepts and proficiency indicators to support the development of your customized study guide. You will repeat these steps for each knowledge area and sub-competency until you have completed your review of the SHRM BASK.

We present examples of applying this approach to a knowledge area and a behavioral competency and sub-competency in Section 3.

How to Study Key Concepts

Key concepts are the most straightforward component of the SHRM BASK with respect to identifying information to build your study guide. They specify the complete list of topics that will be covered on both the SHRM-CP and SHRM-SCP exams. Figuring out what you need to know and what is tested on the exam is an excellent place to start.

How to Study Proficiency Indicators

Proficiency indicators are a bit more complicated to use for building a study guide. They require more self-reflection and analysis than key concepts. As noted previously, proficiency indicators reflect what competent HR behavior and performance look like in practice. That is, they define high-level HR best practices according to their associated knowledge area or behavioral sub-competency. We present some recommended steps to analyze a proficiency indicator to help build your study guide.

Before we get started, you need to be clear which exam you are preparing for: SHRM-CP or SHRM-SCP. Remember that proficiency indicators are differentiated by which exam you will take. Indicators for all HR professionals will be assessed on the SHRM-CP exam, whereas indicators for advanced HR professionals will be assessed on the SHRM-SCP exam.

Important Reminder

When reviewing the SHRM BASK, it is important to remember that the competency model reflects expectations for the HR profession in general and not your specific HR role or those of others in your organization. It is easy to get confused about what you do (or have done) in your career and what is considered proficient for the HR professional at your level in general.

Depending on your current job and past experiences, you may not have had the opportunity to perform or experience everything specified in the SHRM BASK, and that is okay. You don't have to have experience in all the areas presented to be eligible to take the exam. They are a guide as to what is expected of an HR professional at your level.

QUICK TIP
Recommended Steps to Identifying Key Concepts to Study

1. Review the list of key concepts for the particular functional knowledge area or behavioral competency of interest.

2. Ask yourself the following questions:

   » Which concepts do I know extremely well?

   » Which concepts am I only familiar with at a superficial level?

   » Which concepts do I have limited to no knowledge about?

3. Take note of with which key concepts you have only some or no familiarity. These are good targets to add to your study guide. It can also be useful to refresh on the key concepts that you think you know extremely well.

4. Think about how the key concept could be tested with KIs, according to the four cognitive levels (i.e., recall, understanding, problem-solving, and critical evaluation).

   » What are the facts about this key concept?

   » How would I demonstrate understanding of this key concept?

   » What types of problems could I be expected to solve that would rely on this key concept?

   » Can I predict outcomes under varying conditions?

QUICK TIP
Recommended Steps to Understanding Proficiency Indicators for the SHRM-CP exam

1. Review the proficiency indicators for *All HR Professionals* for a particular knowledge area or behavioral sub-competency of interest.

2. Ask yourself the following questions:

    » Which indicators resonate with experiences I have had during my HR career?

    » Which indicators am I familiar with because I have observed others perform them?

    » Which indicators am I unfamiliar with altogether?

3. As you did with the key concepts, take note of which proficiency indicators fall into each category. They will all require some further analysis to support your test preparation.

4. For each proficiency indicator, think about which key concepts are valuable for supporting the proficient performance of this indicator. Linking key concepts to proficiency indicators can aid your understanding of different applications for a key concept and scenarios you could encounter on the exam in KIs and SJIs.

5. For each proficiency indicator, identify the HR best practices for this indicator.

    » Think about what steps are involved in satisfying the proficiency indicator.

    » Identify any additional key concepts that you didn't initially select that could now be useful to study more closely. Go back to the recommended steps for using key concepts to determine if these need to go on your study guide list.

    » Consider that you may know the ways that you have handled this proficiency indicator in the past and these responses may have been effective for your given situation, but they may not actually reflect HR best practices.

    » Take note of the situations you have encountered or witnessed that have involved this proficiency indicator as these could be reflected on the exam.

    » Identify and add any HR best practices and proficiency indicators to your study guide list.

    » Can I predict outcomes under varying conditions?

Section 3

Using the **SHRM BASK** to Prepare for the **SHRM-CP** Exam

In this section, we take what we learned in Section 2 and apply it to the HR Expertise areas and behavioral competencies, selecting an example of each to highlight how you can leverage the SHRM BASK in your test preparation. This process will help you figure out what you need to study and understand the nuance underlying the SHRM BASK.

HR Expertise Example: Organizational Effectiveness & Development

Using the recommended steps presented in Section 2, let's go through an example using the ***Organizational Effectiveness & Development*** knowledge area within the **Organization** knowledge domain. This technical knowledge area refers to the overall structure and functionality of the organization and involves (1) measurement of long- and short-term effectiveness and growth of people and processes and (2) implementation of necessary organizational change initiatives.

Note that the material presented under the HR Expertise technical competency will only be assessed with KIs.

Key Concepts

Because key concepts define testable content material, especially for KIs, we will start here and then move to proficiency indicators, selecting one example of each to examine more closely.

Step 1. Review Key Concepts
The first step is the most basic: Read the list of key concepts and the examples associated with the concepts. The key concepts for *Organizational Effectiveness & Development* are as follows:

» Group dynamics,

» Organizational design structures and approaches, and

» Organizational analysis.

Step 2. Categorize Key Concepts According to Level of Familiarity

For each key concept, categorize them according to familiarity: extremely familiar, somewhat familiar (i.e., superficial knowledge), and limited to no familiarity. Make sure to review the associated examples as there may be some for which you may have more or less knowledge.

Step 3. Take Note of Any Key Concepts Requiring Additional Study

Any key concepts that fall into the latter two categories of somewhat or no familiarity are targets for further investigation and study. Identify these topics for your personal study guide. Recognize, of course, that a refresher review of any key concepts that you are already very comfortable with is a good idea to ensure your knowledge is up to date with the literature.

For this example, we will select the key concept of **group dynamics**.

» Examples of this key concept include *intergroup and intragroup; group formation; identity; cohesion; structure; influence on behavior; conflict; forming, storming, norming, and performing.*

Step 4. Identify How the Key Concept May Be Assessed with a KI

When studying the various key concepts, it is easy to stick to learning the facts about the concept such as the details associated with a particular theory or the steps involved in a process. Think about how you might use your knowledge to demonstrate your understanding, ability to solve situational problems, or predict outcomes.

Returning to our example, how might *group dynamics* be tested with a stand-alone KI?

To demonstrate how group dynamics can be assessed differently, Figures 3.1 and 3.2 present example KIs that reflect understanding and problem-solving, respectively.

Although both KI examples address group dynamics concepts and present example situations, the understanding item asks the test taker to assess the example and identify the theoretical term reflected in the example. The problem-solving KI, on the other hand, requires the test taker to take what they know about group dynamics and identify an effective solution to achieve the desired result of mitigating inter-unit conflict.

A manager is responsible for two teams that work in different locations. The manager wants to promote a more cohesive culture, but the teams continually disagree on key process issues. Which term is this an example of? A. Intergroup conflict B. Personality differences C. Power distance D. Status differences	**Key:** C, Power distance **Description:** This item reflects an understanding of the concept of power distance, which refers to power inequalities among individuals and groups. The item reflects understanding because it presents a situation that asks the test taker to identify the concept being depicted in the example situation.

Figure 3.1. Understanding KI for Group Dynamics

Following a recent merger, an operations executive informs the HR manager that key business units are in conflict over the value each group brings to the organization. Which activity should the HR manager recommend to the executive to address this?

A. Form a committee with leaders of different units to identify differences.

B. Hold a teambuilding activity with members from different units to form working partnerships.

C. Engage business unit leaders in direct communication to change the perceptions of other leaders.

D. Hold an all-hands meeting to promote a shared understanding of organizational values.

Key: D, Hold an all-hands meeting to promote a shared understanding of organizational values.

Description: This item is classified as problem-solving because it asks the test taker to assess the situation presented in the item and identify the best course of action given knowledge of group dynamics.

Figure 3.2. Problem-Solving KI for Group Dynamics

Proficiency Indicators

Proficiency indicators reflect HR best practices related to the HR technical competency or behavioral sub-competencies and can best be leveraged to identify context for situational prompts. As noted previously, they tend to be defined at the highest level of proficiency without dictating how the action can be accomplished. As a result, further analysis is required to support building a personal study guide.

Let's continue with our example of the functional knowledge area of *Organizational Effectiveness & Development* and apply the recommended process for one proficiency indicator.

Step 1. Review Proficiency Indicators for All HR Professionals
For the SHRM-CP exam, review the proficiency indicators listed for *All HR Professionals*. The proficiency indicators for *Organizational Effectiveness & Development* are as follows:

» Ensures that key documents and systems (examples include job postings, job descriptions, and performance management systems) accurately reflect workforce activities.

» Supports change initiatives to increase the effectiveness of HR systems and processes.

» Identifies areas in the organization's structures, processes, and procedures that need change.

» Recommends methods to eliminate barriers to organizational effectiveness and development.

» Collects and analyzes data on organizational performance and the value of HR initiatives to the organization.

Step 2. Categorize Proficiency Indicators According to Level of Familiarity

For each proficiency indicator, ask yourself the following questions regarding your familiarity with them as a result of your HR career to date:

» Which indicators resonate with experiences I have had during my HR career? (Extremely Familiar)

» Which indicators am I only familiar with because I have observed others perform them? (Somewhat Familiar)

» Which indicators am I unfamiliar with altogether? (Limited to No Familiarity)

Categorize the indicators according to familiarity: extremely familiar, somewhat familiar (i.e., superficial knowledge), and limited to no familiarity.

Step 3. Take Note of Any Proficiency Indicators Requiring Additional Study

Take note of which proficiency indicators fall into each familiarity category. Unlike key concepts, they will all require further analysis to support your test preparation.

Step 4. Link Proficiency Indicators to Key Concepts

For each proficiency indicator, think about which key concepts are valuable for supporting the proficient performance of this proficiency indicator. Linking key concepts to proficiency indicators can aid your understanding of different applications for a key concept and scenarios you could encounter on the exam.

For example, let's look at the proficiency indicator, *recommends methods to eliminate barriers to organizational effectiveness and development.* What key concepts are relevant to this indicator?

» *Group dynamics* assuming that there are issues with organizational cohesion and group performance, and

» *Organizational design structures and approaches* because these could influence the methods that might be taken to eliminate structural barriers to effectiveness.

The problem-solving KI example presented in Figure 3.2 effectively demonstrates how a proficiency indicator can be leveraged to identify a context for applying a key concept. For convenience, we re-present the stem with an explanation of the linkage in Figure 3.3.

Step 5. Identify HR Best Practices

As written, there is a great deal of nuance in how a proficiency indicator can be accomplished or performed. Each proficiency indicator, as a result, can be broken down into lower-level components, each of which may have their own set of recommended best practices. Examining the lower-level steps or components will help you identify additional contextual situations that you may encounter on the exam, as well as additional key concepts that you may need to consider for review.

Item Stem	Linkage Explanation
Following a recent merger, an operations executive informs the HR manager that key business units are in conflict over the value each group brings to the organization. Which activity should the HR manager recommend to the executive to address this?	The item presents a situation and asks the test taker to recommend a method to eliminate an identified barrier to the organization's effectiveness. This item requires knowledge of the key concept (*group dynamics*) and directly links to the proficiency indicator (*recommends methods to eliminate barriers to organizational effectiveness and development*).

Figure 3.3. Key Concept Linkage Example: Technical Knowledge Area Proficiency Indicator

For each proficiency indicator

1. Think about how this proficiency indicator can be accomplished. What steps, factors, or other considerations are involved in satisfying the proficiency indicator?

   For this example proficiency indicator (*recommends methods to eliminate barriers to organizational effectiveness and development)* lower-level steps might include reviews organizational performance analysis for trends and patterns, consults with subject matter experts to identify potential solutions, or assesses merits of different solutions.

2. Identify any additional key concepts that you didn't initially select that could now be useful. Go back to the recommended steps for using key concepts to determine if these need to go on your study guide list.

   For example, if a lower-level step is reviewing an organizational performance report, you may want to add the key concept, organizational analysis, to your list of key concepts to study (if you haven't already).

3. Consider that you may know the ways that you have handled this proficiency indicator in the past and these responses may have been effective for your given situation, but they may not actually reflect HR best practices.

4. Take note of the situations you have encountered or witnessed that have involved this proficiency indicator as these could be reflected on the exam.

5. Identify and add any HR best practices and proficiency indicators to your study guide list as needed.

Behavioral Competency Example: Relationship Management

Now let's do the same thing using a behavioral competency as the starting point, using *Relationship Management* from the *Interpersonal* cluster. Relationship Management is defined as the KSAOs needed to create and maintain a network of professional contacts within and outside the organization, to build and maintain relationships, to work as an effective member of a team, and to manage conflict while supporting the organization.

As evident in Figure 2.2, key concepts are specified at the behavioral competency level. As a result, we will begin with the behavioral competency when reviewing key concepts and eventually narrow down to a sub-competency when examining the proficiency indicators.

Key Concepts

As we did for HR Expertise, we will present how to use the recommended approach, focusing on one key concept for demonstration.

Step 1. Review Key Concepts

Read the list of key concepts and the examples associated with the concepts. The key concepts for *Relationship Management* are as follows:

» Types of conflict;

» Conflict resolution strategies;

» Negotiation tactics, strategies, and styles; and

» Trust-building techniques.

Step 2. Categorize Key Concepts According to Level of Familiarity

For each key concept, categorize them according to familiarity: extremely familiar, somewhat familiar (i.e., superficial knowledge), and limited to no familiarity. Make sure to review the associated examples as there may be some for which you may have more or less knowledge.

Step 3. Take Note of Any Key Concepts Requiring Additional Study

Any key concepts that fall into the latter two categories of somewhat or no familiarity are targets for further investigation and study. Identify these topics for your personal study guide. Recognize, of course, that a refresher review of any key concepts that you are already very comfortable with is a good idea to ensure your knowledge is up to date with the literature.

For this example, we will select the key concept of *conflict resolution strategies.* Examples of this key concept include accommodation, collaboration, compromise, competition, and avoidance.

Step 4. Identify How the Key Concept May Be Assessed with a KI

Think about how you might use your knowledge to demonstrate your understanding and ability to solve situational problems, or predict outcomes.

Returning to our example, how might *conflict resolution strategies* be tested with a stand-alone KI?

To demonstrate how conflict resolution strategies can be assessed differently, Figures 3.4 and 3.5 present examples of KIs that reflect recall and problem-solving, respectively.

Which give-and-take decision-making process involves independent parties with different preferences? A. Diversity management B. Bargaining C. Conflict resolution D. Negotiation	**Key**: D, Negotiation **Description**: Negotiation by definition is a give-and-take process designed to help two or more parties come to a decision or resolution. For this item, the test taker is required to simply identify the term corresponding to the definition presented in the item stem and it is therefore classified as *recall*.

Figure 3.4. Recall KI for Conflict Resolution Strategies

A CEO wants to resolve a conflict between two executives without involving HR in the initial conversation. Which action should the HR manager suggest the CEO take to address this situation? A. Meet both employees in person and document the details for HR to review. B. Follow the company's code of conduct and conflict resolution policy. C. Refer the case to HR to explore options to resolve the interpersonal conflict. D. Consider mediation services to resolve the conflict.	**Key**: A, Meet both employees in person and document the details for HR to review. **Description**: This item presents a situation and requires the test taker to identify an effective response to resolve the problem. In this case, an effective first step, and recommended best practice, is for the CEO to meet with both employees and document the details carefully. The other response options may also be effective responses but do not address the detail that the CEO would like to avoid involving HR at the outset.

Figure 3.5. Problem-Solving KI for Conflict Resolution Strategies

Although both KI examples address conflict resolution strategies, the recall item straightforwardly focuses on the definition of key terminology and does not require the test taker to do anything further than remember the information. The problem-solving KI, on the other hand, requires the test taker to take what they know about conflict resolution strategies and identify an effective solution to achieve the desired result before involving HR directly.

Proficiency Indicators

Continuing with *Relationship Management*, let's look at the proficiency indicators and follow the recommended approach identified in Section 2. However, as noted previously, remember that proficiency indicators are specified under sub-competencies. For this exercise, we will focus on the sub-competency of *Conflict Management*, which focuses on the management and resolution of conflicts by identifying areas of common interest among the parties in conflict.

Step 1. Review Proficiency Indicators for All HR Professionals

For the SHRM-CP exam, review the proficiency indicators listed for *All HR Professionals.* The proficiency indicators for *Conflict Management* are as follows:

» Resolves and/or mediates conflicts in a respectful, appropriate, and impartial manner, and refers them to a higher level when warranted.

» Identifies and addresses the underlying causes of conflict.

» Facilitates difficult interactions among employees to achieve optimal outcomes.

» Encourages productive and respectful task-related conflict and uses it to facilitate change.

» Serves as a positive role model for productive conflict.

» Identifies and resolves conflict that is counterproductive or harmful.

Step 2. Categorize Proficiency Indicators According to Level of Familiarity

For each proficiency indicator, ask yourself the following questions regarding your familiarity with them as a result of your HR career to date:

» Which indicators resonate with experiences I have had during my HR career? (Extremely Familiar)

» Which indicators am I only familiar with because I have observed others perform them? (Somewhat Familiar)

» Which indicators am I unfamiliar with altogether? (Limited to No Familiarity)

Categorize the indicators according to familiarity: extremely familiar, somewhat familiar (i.e., superficial knowledge), and limited to no familiarity.

Step 3. Take Note of Any Proficiency Indicators Requiring Additional Study

Take note of which proficiency indicators fall into each familiarity category. Unlike for key concepts, they will all require further analysis to support your test preparation.

Step 4. Link Proficiency Indicators to Key Concepts

For each proficiency indicator, think about which key concepts are valuable for supporting proficient performance of this indicator. Linking key concepts to proficiency indicators can aid your understanding of different applications for a key concept and scenarios you could encounter on the exam.

For the indicator, **resolves and/or mediates conflicts in a respectful and impartial manner, and refers them to a higher level when warranted**, for example, what key concepts are relevant to this indicator?

» *Types of conflict* because knowing the type of conflict may impact the method of resolution,

» *Conflict resolution strategies* because this indicator clearly focuses on the act of resolving the conflict, and

» *Trust-building techniques* because effective conflict resolution typically involves employing the techniques presented as examples.

The problem-solving KI example presented in Figure 3.5 effectively demonstrates how a proficiency indicator can be leveraged to identify a context for applying a key concept. For convenience, we re-present the stem with an explanation of the linkage in Figure 3.6.

Item Stem	Linkage Explanation
A CEO wants to resolve a conflict between two executives without involving HR in the initial conversation. Which action should the HR manager suggest the CEO take to address this situation?	The item presents a situation and asks the test taker to recommend an initial step to address the situation before involving HR. This item requires knowledge of the key concept (conflict resolution strategies) and directly links to the proficiency indicator (resolves and/or mediates conflicts in a respectful and impartial manner, and refers them to a higher level when warranted).

Figure 3.6. Key Concept Linkage Example: Sub-Competency Proficiency Indicator

Behavioral sub-competency proficiency indicators can also provide situational context for SJIs. The next examples (Figure 3.7) showcase two SJIs based on the same scenario, both focusing on the sub-competency, Conflict Management.

Step 5. Identify HR Best Practices

This step is focused on doing a deeper dive into understanding the best practices associated with a proficiency indicator. Doing this analysis will help you identify additional contextual situations that you may encounter on the exam, as well as additional key concepts that you may need to consider for additional review.

For each proficiency indicator

1. Think about how this proficiency can be accomplished. What steps, factors, or other considerations are involved in satisfying the proficiency indicator?

   For this example indicator (resolves and/or mediates conflicts in a respectful, appropriate and impartial manner, and refers them to a higher level when warranted), lower-level steps might include: communicates with the parties in conflict to address and schedule meeting(s), identifies appropriate conflict resolution strategies, prepares for the conflict resolution meeting, and reviews policies regarding conflict management.

2. Identify any additional key concepts that you didn't initially select that could now be useful. Go back to the recommended steps for using key concepts to determine if these need to go on your study guide list.

SJI Scenario
The director at a telecommunications company receives several complaints about a manager who works on the director's team. The complaints allege that the manager demonstrates favoritism when interacting with direct reports. Moreover, the director has observed on multiple occasions that the manager does not get along well with the other managers on the team and is concerned that the manager consistently fails to meet performance objectives. The director has spoken to the manager on several occasions about all of these issues but has not observed any improvement. Both the director and manager approach the HR manager separately to complain about the other. The director complains about the manager's behaviors and poor performance, and the manager complains that the director is unfairly criticizing the manager's performance.

Conflict Management SJI 1	
Which action should the HR manager take to address the issue of the manager not getting along with the other managers? A. Conduct a team-building event with all managers that highlights their shared goals. B. Collect performance feedback from the other managers and privately share it with the manager. C. Ask the director to be more supportive of the manager so that it sets a good example for the other managers. D. Require all managers to meet regularly to discuss shared objectives and company goals.	**Key**: A, Conduct a team-building event with all managers that highlights their shared goals.

Conflict Management SJI 2	
Which action should the HR manager take to address the conflict between the director and the manager? A. Suggest to the manager that explaining to the director how the manager feels may improve the situation. B. Discuss with the manager the possibility of transferring to a new role under a different supervisor. C. Meet with the manager and director separately to discuss the complaints and identify possible solutions. D. Ask the director to share data with the HR manager that confirms the manager is not meeting performance objectives.	**Key**: C, Meet with the manager and director separately to discuss the complaints and identify possible solutions.

Figure 3.7. SJIs for Conflict Management

For example, your initial review of the proficiency indicator may not have signaled that the conflict required negotiation tactics but now you do. Therefore, you may want to add the key concept (negotiation tactics, strategies and styles) to your list of key concepts to study (if you haven't already).

3. Consider that you may know the ways that you have handled this proficiency indicator in the past and these responses may have been effective for your given situation, but they may not actually reflect HR best practices.

4. Take note of the situations you have encountered of witnessed that have involved this proficiency indicator as these could be reflected on the exam.

5. Identify and add any HR best practices and proficiency indicators to your study guide list, as needed.

Let's Practice! Twenty SHRM-CP Practice Items and Answers

Now, let's apply what we have learned over the past two sections regarding the use of the SHRM BASK as a preparation tool combined with this set of twenty practice items. Each of these items was previously administered on the SHRM-CP exam as a scored test item. This practice item list is not reflective of the entire blueprint that is used to build the SHRM-CP exams. In other words, these practice items are not a mini-exam, and they do not represent all knowledge or behavioral areas tested on the exams.

Separated by item type:

» **Section 1** contains a total of six KIs and foundational knowledge items,

» **Section 2** section contains eight SJIs, and

» **Section 3** section contains another set of six KIs and foundational knowledge items.

The items will give you a flavor of how the questions are structured on the exam and allow you to practice your testing-taking strategies as you answer them. Additionally, you will see how items are linked to the SHRM BASK, difficulty rating, and the answer key and rationale accompanying the items.

Later in this book, you will have access to an additional set of fifty SHRM-CP KIs and SJIs for practice. This set of items will not initially include the SHRM BASK linkage, difficulty rating, or answer keys. The purpose of these items is to test yourself as if the items were actual test items. The SHRM BASK alignment, difficulty ratings, answer key responses, and rationales will be provided following the fifty practice items.

One very important caution: do not assume that the ability to answer this set of fifty practice items correctly equates to a passing score on the certification exam. Similarly, do not use the results to predict how well you will do on the certification exam itself. Combined, these lists compose just over half of the number of items on the SHRM-CP exam. Also, these practice items do not fully cover all of the competency clusters and knowledge domains that are represented on the real exams. For these reasons, the practice items are intended to give a preview of the structure and format of test questions. It is not appropriate to use results to predict an outcome on your exam, and doing well on these practice items will not guarantee a passing result on your exam.

For examinees who plan to test outside of the United States, you will see questions about U.S. Employment Law & Regulations. Questions in this functional area do not appear on exams for examinees who reside outside of the United States. If you reside outside the United States and plan to take your exam outside of the United States, omit these questions and adjust your timing accordingly.

Section 1: This section is composed of six knowledge items (KIs).

1. The accounting employees complain to management that the operations employees are not responding to communications and missing key deadlines. The operations employees claim that accounting employees miscommunicated deadlines and are spreading misinformation. This is an example of which type of conflict?

    A. Environmental

    B. Interpersonal

    C. Internal

    D. Intergroup

Domain	Sub-Competency	Difficulty	Key
Organization	Organizational Effectiveness & Development	Somewhat Hard	D

Rationale

"Intergroup" is the correct answer because intergroup conflict occurs when two or more organizational groups or teams disagree.

2. An HR manager is designing techniques to increase product quality by decreasing defects in a company's processes. What quality assurance technique is the HR manager using?

    A. Gap analysis

    B. Six Sigma

    C. Benchmarking

    D. Cost benefit analysis

Domain	Sub-Competency	Difficulty	Key
Workplace	Risk Management	Somewhat Easy	B

Rationale

"Six Sigma" is correct because Six Sigma is a set of techniques and tools for process improvement aimed at increasing quality by decreasing defects in processes.

3. What level of the Kirkpatrick Model evaluates the degree to which participants perceive the training as relevant to their jobs?

   A. Reaction

   B. Learning

   C. Behavior

   D. Results

Domain	Sub-Competency	Difficulty	Key
People	Learning & Development	Hard	A
Rationale			
"Reaction" is correct because per the Kirkpatrick Model, Level 1 evaluates the degree to which participants find the training favorable, engaging, and relevant to their jobs.			

4. What key action should an employee belonging to a marginalized group take who wants to move into a senior-level role in a company where a high percentage of employees belonging to marginalized groups are in entry-level positions and middle management?

   A. Identify and proactively enlist sponsors and mentors.

   B. Give a high rating during a self-performance appraisal.

   C. Inform management about performance highlights.

   D. Dedicate more hours to the employee's current role.

Domain	Sub-Competency	Difficulty	Key
Leadership	Inclusion & Diversity	Easy	A
Rationale			
"Identify and proactively enlist sponsors and mentors" is correct because the employee should be proactive in identifying and enlisting sponsors and mentors to help break the glass ceiling at this company. The employee should not wait until the relationships are created for them, but reach out to others to network and learn from them and make their career ambitions known. These relationships can provide positive benefits for both the employee and their sponsors or mentors.			

5. Which conflict resolution styles are characterized by high assertiveness?

   A. Competing and avoiding

B.   Avoiding and accommodating

C.   Collaborating and competing

D.   Collaborating and accommodating

Domain	Sub-Competency	Difficulty	Key
Interpersonal	Relationship Management	Somewhat Hard	C
Rationale			

"Collaborating and competing" is correct because the Thomas-Kilman Collaborating and Conflict Management Instrument (TKI) characterizes the Collaborating and Competing resolution styles as being high in assertiveness.

6.   Which action should an HR specialist take to prepare for new employees at a company that is scheduled to hire a large number of seasonal workers?

A.   Ensure an onboarding plan is in place.

B.   Review budget for an increase of payroll.

C.   Plan a formal orientation event.

D.   Increase perks and incentive pay.

Domain	Sub-Competency	Difficulty	Key
Organization	Workforce Management	Somewhat Easy	A
Rationale			

"Ensure an onboarding plan is in place" is correct because it's important to set seasonal staff up for success with a solid onboarding experience. Providing seasonal staff the resources and tools they need upfront allows them to build better working relations and establish trust in the company.

Section 2: This section is composed of sixteen situational judgment items (SJIs).

The following scenario accompanies the next three items.

A manufacturing company is struggling to retain employees across multiple positions. The employees' average salaries are below the market average for all positions, and the company does not have a standardized starting wage for new employees at each position level. The CEO tasks the HR manager to review the compensation system for improvements. Under the current system, each selected candidate is offered a salary based on the level of success the hiring manager predicts their future job performance will achieve.

If the candidate rejects the initial offer, the hiring manager counteroffers with a higher salary. Recently, employees have begun openly discussing their salaries, and many have learned that they have lower salaries than co-workers who have the same job responsibilities. The pay discrepancy has resulted in increased turnover, low morale, and decreased productivity. Some of the employees have requested meetings with the HR manager to discuss their salaries.

7. How should the HR manager approach establishing a standardized, impartial minimum salary for each position given the current employees' inconsistent pay ranges?

   A. Establish a minimum salary equal to the current median salary for each position.

   B. Require that hiring managers offer the same salary to all candidates.

   C. Perform a study comparing the salaries of similar jobs at other companies.

   D. Conduct a job analysis for each position to determine acceptable salary ranges.

Domain	Sub-Competency	Difficulty	Key
Business	Business Acumen	Easy	D

8. The HR manager recommends the CEO authorize wage increases for high-performing employees to prevent turnover. Which action should the HR manager take to persuade the CEO to raise salaries?

   A. Tell the CEO that the morale of high-performing employees has a substantial influence on other employees.

   B. Conduct a cost-benefit analysis that accounts for expected effects on turnover and productivity.

   C. Prepare a report highlighting several accomplishments of high-performing employees to share with the CEO.

   D. Hold a focus group with high-performing employees and the CEO to discuss employee salaries.

Domain	Sub-Competency	Difficulty	Key
Interpersonal	Communication	Easy	B

9. A hiring manager admits to offering a lower initial salary to some applicants based solely on age. Which action should the HR manager take to most comprehensively correct the manager's behavior?

   A. Recommend the hiring manager apologize to all affected employees.

B.   Ask the CEO to formally discipline the hiring manager.

C.   Tell the hiring manager that continuing this practice would be bad for morale.

D.   Require all offer letters be approved by HR prior to delivery.

Domain	Sub-Competency	Difficulty	Key
Leadership	Inclusion & Diversity	Somewhat Easy	D

The following scenario accompanies the next two items.

A midsize organization is dealing with a retention problem. Specifically, many employees are leaving within one to three years of being hired. The HR VP recently requested that the HR manager find the root cause and offer solutions to the executive team. The HR manager reviewed exit interviews and noticed that most of the employees who were leaving did not feel engaged after they were hired. Many reported that they did not understand the company culture and did not see a clear career path for themselves to grow and advance within the company. They felt they were not given sufficient support in their first few weeks and had to teach themselves about company procedures and expectations. The HR manager determines that the onboarding program must be completely updated.

10.   Which is the best way for the HR manager to introduce new employees to the company culture?

A.   Launch a job rotation program for employees to complete during their first year.

B.   Write a report explaining the company's culture for new employees to read.

C.   Create a frequently asked questions page on the company's website.

D.   Host informal lunches with new employees and leadership to discuss the culture.

Domain	Sub-Competency	Difficulty	Key
Interpersonal	Communication	Easy	D

11.   Which is the most effective way for the HR manager to measure the success of the new onboarding system?

A.   Compare turnover rates of new employees before and after the new system was implemented.

B.   Conduct interviews with the managers of the new employees to ask about the success of the system.

C.   Invite employees to submit complaints about the new system and review them weekly.

D.   Analyze performance appraisal ratings before and after the new system was launched.

Domain	Sub-Competency	Difficulty	Key
Business	Analytical Aptitude	Easy	A

The following scenario accompanies the next three items.

An employee for a small architectural design firm is required to work in another country for six months. Consequently, the employee is issued a corporate credit card to cover work-related expenses. Historically, before being issued corporate credit cards, all employees have been required to sign an agreement stating the card is only for business-related expenses and never for personal use. However, this employee signs the newest edition of the agreement, which also states that a breach of the agreement will result in a deduction of wages and possible termination. Five months into the employee's international assignment, the company receives a larger-than-expected monthly credit card bill. An audit of the credit card statement reveals the employee spent a large amount on personal expenses, including clothing and electronics.

12.   What is the first action the HR manager should take after receiving the results of the audit?

A.   Suspend the employee's access to the credit card to prevent further misuse of the card.

B.   Request the employee submit all receipts relating to the use of the corporate credit card.

C.   Contact the employee to determine the reason the purchases were made.

D.   Demand that the employee immediately repay the debt or face disciplinary action.

Domain	Sub-Competency	Difficulty	Key
Leadership	Ethical Practice	Somewhat Hard	C

13. The HR manager requests an audit of all of the company's corporate credit card accounts going back three years. The audit reveals that several employees have misused company credit cards. What should the HR manager do to improve ethical behavior within the firm?

    A. Request that employees write a report explaining their reasons for not adhering to the policy.

    B. Enforce strict disciplinary actions on each of the policy violations that occurred in the past three years.

    C. Task individual managers with ensuring that direct reports understand and abide by the company policy.

    D. Implement a multi-level approval process for monthly credit card transactions for each department.

Domain	Sub-Competency	Difficulty	Key
Leadership	Ethical Practice	Somewhat Easy	C

14. The HR manager decides to monitor their corporate credit card and discovers an unauthorized personal purchase made last year. Suspecting this was a mistake, how should the HR manager correct the error?

    A. Follow the required procedures to repay the company for the unauthorized purchase.

    B. Meet with the firm's senior management team to notify them and explain the situation.

    C. Use a personal credit card to pay for business-related expenses equal to the amount of the unauthorized charge.

    D. Ask the CEO for forgiveness based on the HR manager's previous record of highly ethical behavior.

Domain	Sub-Competency	Difficulty	Key
Leadership	Ethical Practice	Somewhat Easy	A

Section 3: This section is composed of six knowledge items (KIs).

15. A chief human resource officer is evaluating the company's total rewards strategy after experiencing higher-than-normal turnover due to a global shift in work styles. Which approach should the company take to retain and attract talent?

    A. Reinforce policies and procedures.

    B. Participate in salary surveys.

    C. Offer flexible schedule options.

    D. Eliminate voluntary benefit plans.

Domain	Sub-Competency	Difficulty	Key
People	Total Rewards	Easy	C
Rationale			
"Offer flexible schedule options" is correct because flexible work options are the highest demand of workers in recent years. Offering various options also meets the needs of a diverse workforce.			

16. A company has offered to give any employee forty hours of paid time off throughout the year if the employee uses that time to volunteer with a local charity. Which best describes the company's responsibility to society?

    A. Operational

    B. Ethical

    C. Legal

    D. Financial

Domain	Sub-Competency	Difficulty	Key
Workplace	Corporate Social Responsibility	Somewhat Easy	B
Rationale			
"Ethical" is correct because this refers to a company's commitment to business practices that are right and fair for all stakeholders.			

17. In which way do employer brand and employee value proposition (EVP) differ?

    A. Employer brand is the company's reputation in the market; EVP is the promise of the employment experience between employer and employee.

    B. Employer brand is applied to the external audience or future employees; EVP is applied to the internal audience or current employees.

    C. Employer brand is the experience within the context of the overall EVP; EVP is the sum total of how people perceive the organization.

    D. Employer brand is the marketing strategy led by recruitment; EVP is the online presence of the company influenced by marketing efforts.

Domain	Sub-Competency	Difficulty	Key
People	**Talent Acquisition**	**Somewhat Hard**	**A**

Rationale

"Employer brand is the company's reputation in the market; EVP is the promise of the employment experience between employer and employee" is correct because the two differ in that the employer brand is the company's reputation in the talent market the company is seeking to influence and the EVP is the promise of the employment experience between the employer and employee and is within the context of the employer brand.

18. An HR manager is tasked with hiring a high-performance workforce with problem-solving skills and the ability to deal with new, uncertain, and complex situations. Which diversity should the HR manager target?

    A. Ethnic

    B. Cognitive

    C. Cultural

    D. Generational

Domain	Sub-Competency	Difficulty	Key
Interpersonal	**Global Mindset**	**Easy**	**B**

Rationale

"Cognitive" is correct because it is the difference in perspective or information processing styles and focuses on thinking.

19. An HR manager is considering a new HRIS and planning to outsource payroll since the company does not currently have a payroll specialist. What outsourcing arrangement is the HR manager utilizing?

    A. Business process outsourcing (BPO)

    B. Single-source outsourcing

    C. Professional employer organizations

    D. Shared services

Domain	Sub-Competency	Difficulty	Key
Organization	**Structure of the HR Function**	**Hard**	**A**

Rationale

"Business process outsourcing (BPO)" is correct because BPO consists of outsourcing a single business task, as well as the software service.

20. How does the Patient Protection and Affordable Care Act impact companies that utilize part-time employees?

    A. Companies that offer health insurance to full-time employees are required to offer health insurance to part-time employees.

    B. Companies are not required to offer health insurance to employees who work less than 40 hours per week.

    C. Companies whose part-time employees purchase coverage from a state health insurance exchange incur a penalty.

    D. Companies are not required to offer health insurance to employees who work less than 30 hours per week.

Domain	Sub-Competency	Difficulty	Key
Workplace	U.S. Employment Law & Regulations	Somewhat Easy	D

Rationale

"Companies are not required to offer health insurance to employees who work less than 30 hours per week" is correct because part-time employees used to be considered those individuals who worked less than thirty-five hours or less than forty hours a week, but this is changed to under thirty hours a week under this act. Companies that offer health insurance to full-time employees are not required to offer health insurance to part-time employees. Companies also will not incur a penalty if part-time employees purchase their health coverage from a state health insurance exchange.

Section 4

The SHRM-CP Exam Blueprint

Not only does SHRM provide the potential content areas for the SHRM-CP exam in the SHRM BASK, SHRM also provides the actual breakdown of the numbers of exam items in the different content areas (Figure 4.1).

When measuring the three clusters of behavioral competencies, the exam includes close to equal representation from the different areas:

» **Leadership:** 17% of overall exam items,

» **Business:** 16.5% of overall exam items, and

» **Interpersonal:** 16.5% of overall exam items.

In addition, for the HR knowledge domains, the People and Organization domains have more items than the Workplace domain. This difference is not surprising given the fact that Workplace only includes four functional areas, while People and Organization both include five functional areas.

» **People:** 18% of overall exam items,

» **Organization:** 18% of overall exam items, and

» **Workplace:** 14% of overall exam items.

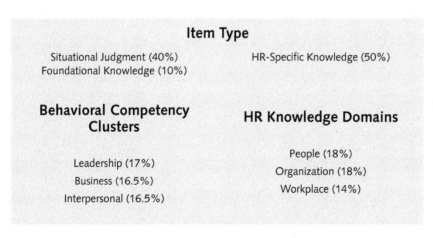

Figure 4.1. Distribution of Exam Items by Content and Exam Type

Self-Assessment for Your Exam Study Plan

Now that you have seen and started interacting with the SHRM BASK, you might feel a bit overwhelmed by the sheer volume of potential exam content. In fact, many SHRM-CP examinees are not sure what they should spend their time focused on and where they should start studying. Remember, the SHRM Learning System is a robust option offering a comprehensive study package complete with pre-tests to assess your knowledge and identify gaps to provide a customized study plan based on your designated exam date.

To help diagnose your stronger and weaker areas and to direct your studying, we have put together this informal self-assessment for you. Note that this is not a true assessment of your knowledge but an informal resource you can use to determine where you need the most help and could benefit most in studying.

As you go through this assessment, try to be honest with yourself about your level of expertise. In many cases, you might not have a good understanding of your own knowledge level. That is okay and completely expected. If you are unsure of the meaning of terms, that is probably an indicator that you are not very knowledgeable in the area.

As a reminder, you can find the complete, complimentary, downloadable version of the SHRM BASK at

> https://www.shrm.org/credentials/certification/exam-preparation/body-of-applied-skills-and-knowledge

Instructions

Read the definition, sub-competencies (for behavioral competencies), key concepts, and proficiency indicators for all HR professionals. This will involve obtaining the full SHRM BASK and using the definitions and various pieces of information in it.

Rate the competencies and knowledge areas based on your level of expertise by placing an X in the appropriate box.

Section 1: Rate Competencies in Leadership Cluster

	Rate Your Level of Expertise		
	Low	Moderate	High
Leadership & Navigation			
Sub-competencies: » Navigating the organization » Vision » Managing HR initiatives » Influence			
Ethical Practice			
Sub-competencies: » Personal integrity » Professional integrity » Ethical agent			
Inclusion & Diversity (I&D)			
Sub-competencies: » Creating an inclusive and diverse culture » Ensuring equity effectiveness » Connecting I&D to organizational performance			

Section 2: Rate Competencies in Interpersonal Cluster

	Rate Your Level of Expertise		
	Low	Moderate	High
Relationship Management			
Sub-competencies: » Networking » Relationship building » Teamwork » Negotiation » Conflict management			
Communication			
Sub-competencies: » Delivering messages » Exchanging organizational information » Listening			
Global Mindset			
Sub-competencies: » Operating in a culturally diverse workplace » Operating in a global environment » Advocating for a culturally inclusive and diverse workplace			

Section 3: Rate Competencies in Business Cluster

	Rate Your Level of Expertise		
	Low	Moderate	High
Business Acumen			
Sub-competencies: » Business and competitive awareness » Business analysis » Strategic alignment			
Consultation			
Sub-competencies: » Evaluating business challenges » Designing HR solutions » Advising on HR solutions » Change management » Service excellence			
Analytical Aptitude			
Sub-competencies: » Data advocate » Data gathering » Data analysis » Evidence-based decision-making			

Section 4: Rate Functional Areas in People Knowledge Domain

	Rate Your Level of Expertise		
	Low	Moderate	High
HR Strategy			
Talent Acquisition			
Employee Engagement & Retention			
Learning & Development			
Total Rewards			

Section 5: Rate Functional Areas in Organization Knowledge Domain

	Rate Your Level of Expertise		
	Low	Moderate	High
Structure of the HR Function			
Organizational Effectiveness & Development			
Workforce Management			
Employee & Labor Relations			
Technology Management			

Section 6: Rate Functional Areas in Workplace Knowledge Domain

	Rate Your Level of Expertise		
	Low	Moderate	High
Managing a Global Workforce			
Risk Management			
Corporate Social Responsibility			
U.S. Employment Law & Regulations			

Scoring the Assessment

Based on your self-ratings of expertise for each behavioral competency or functional area, you can interpret the results based on your ratings of expertise.

Low Expertise = Study Most: These are areas where you have little to no expertise or experience. If you primarily support employee relations and employee engagement, you may need to study most in areas such as talent acquisition or global mindset because you have little to no hands-on experience in this area.

Moderate Expertise = Study Some: These are areas where you have some expertise or experience, but you're not an expert. This could apply if you are a generalist with experience across many (or even most) competencies; you might have a surface-level knowledge of the competency, but you need to spend some time studying to better understand that competency outside of just your role or organization. If you used to work in a specific area but now perform a different set of job duties, this might apply too.

High Expertise = Review Only: These are the areas where you have the most expertise or experience. When you create your study plan, you don't want to spend too much time on these areas. Instead, you'll devote that time to studying the areas where you have more to learn. Note that these might be areas that you prefer to study or are most comfortable with. Because of this, you might have to fight the tendency to spend too much time in areas that you already know.

Interpreting the Assessment

You should now have twenty-three discrete ratings, one for each behavioral competency and functional area. Review your ratings and make notes about the terms, facts, and concepts that you need to learn or know more about so you can include them in your study plan.

It is important to review but not overstudy areas where your knowledge and familiarity with the content is already at a command-and-control level. Instead, focus your study efforts to improve your knowledge on the content with which you are least familiar. This means you should spend the majority of your study time on your study most areas, some time on your study some areas, and only a small amount of time on your review areas. Despite these recommendations, it is also important to note that the pass/fail decision for the exams are based on overall performance, rather than performance in each specific area. As a result, it is possible to pass the exam while performing rather poorly in a small number of subject areas.

Once you have your completed self-assessment, group together the items on your checklist that you can study together to identify study blocks. As you sort items into groups, list the related terms and acronyms. Once you've identified your study blocks, you'll have the outline for your study plan.

Also, we should note that the reference list at the end of the SHRM BASK has many relevant books and other resources that are relevant for learning more about these competencies and functional areas. Remember that it is not a comprehensive list, but these are resources that have been approved by SHRM for item writers to use when creating exam items.

Create a SMART Study Plan

A plan is when a *want to* becomes a *how to*.

After going through the self-assessment and gaining some understanding of the areas of the SHRM-CP where you might need more studying, you should commit to making a plan for preparing for the exam. Although you might be able to follow a generic or informal plan, we know that the act of planning and committing is important for a lot of people to do things that are difficult.

One of the main reasons to focus on the study plan and schedule is the importance of writing things down. You are much more likely to take a commitment more seriously if you document it in a clear way. As such, we encourage you to take advantage of this workbook and use the templates provided in Appendix 2.

Here's how to create a study schedule that will fit into your life:[1]

1. Figure out how many hours you will need to cover everything on your study checklist. SHRM research shows that you should plan on spending at least eighty hours of preparation for the exam—although some people will need significantly more preparation time.

2. Start with the results of the self-assessment and plan your study time accordingly. You should also consider factors such as the extent of your HR experience and how quickly you tend to learn.

3. Determine how much of your time is already committed elsewhere. This will vary greatly between people. You should consider the time you need for family, work, exercise, personal care, and social activities, along with downtime and time for the unexpected, such as illness or a heavier-than-usual workload.

4. Decide how many hours of study time you will have available each week before the exam. If you plan to either form or join a study group or take an exam prep course, identify how many hours each week you will need for those activities. Then divide the remaining time into study sessions.

---

1. Charles Glover, eds., *Ace Your SHRM Certification Exam: The Official SHRM Study Guide for the SHRM-CP® and SHRM-SCP® Exams,* 3rd ed. (Alexandria, VA: SHRM, 2024), 61–63.

5. Determine a specific, achievable goal for each study session and identify the content you will study so you can achieve that goal. Keep in mind that you'll need more study time for some content than for others and build time into your schedule for practice exams so that you can assess what you are learning.

6. Develop a realistic study schedule that shows your study sessions by date and time, the goal for each session, and the content you'll focus on during that session. Try to use this to make a realistic plan for an average of six to eight hours of study per week. Please note that there is no expectation of studying every day; however, it will be a good idea for you to plan on at least three days per week of some studying.

7. Create a week-by-week calendar that includes your scheduled activities for each day during your study period. Include time for family and friends, work (including your commute), scheduled appointments (doctors, dentists, etc.), exercise, and study sessions, study group meetings, and exam prep courses (if any).

Get Started on Your Study Schedule

Now step back and review your calendar:

» How realistic is it?

» Did you leave time for meals and personal care, as well as some downtime so you can rest and relax?

» Did you leave buffer time in case of the unexpected?

If needed, go into your electronic calendar and set aside the time that you assigned to your studies.

Looking for next-level support in creating a study plan and sticking to it? As noted, the SHRM Learning System will identify strengths and gaps in knowledge, allowing more time to prioritize the studying of weaker areas, and while maintaining your areas of strength.

A great feature in the SHRM Learning System is the exam countdown calendar which will generate a customized study approach based on your selected exam date (and your proximity to it) top of mind, so you can plan your studies accordingly. You can pop in and out of the SHRM Learning System when you have a little break, using your phone to access the many quizzes and lessons within the platform.

Section 5

The SHRM-CP Fifty-Item Practice Test

Introduction

This practice test includes fifty items that were previously used on the SHRM-CP exam. These are different items than the ones that are used in the official SHRM study guide, *Ace Your SHRM Certification Exam*, and only include SHRM-CP items.

Similar to the real exam, this practice test is divided into separate sections that are composed of either knowledge items or situational judgment items.

» **Section 1** contains a total of sixteen knowledge and foundational knowledge items,

» **Section 2** contains eighteen situational judgment items, and

» **Section 3** contains another set of sixteen knowledge and foundational knowledge items.

Because this practice test only contains fifty items, it is not entirely representative of the entire blueprint that is used to build the SHRM-CP and SHRM-SCP exams. However, it is generally set up to cover all of the areas in the blueprint. This practice test will give you a taste of how the questions are structured on the exam and allow you to practice your test-taking strategies as you answer them.

To get a better sense of the real exams, SHRM recommends that you take the practice items during a timed period. We suggest you allot one and a half minutes per question (seventy-five minutes total) to gauge your ability to answer questions under the time constraints of the real exams.

One very important caution: do not assume that the ability to answer items on this fifty-item practice test directly correlates to a passing score on the certification exam. This practice test is composed of less than half of the number of items on the SHRM-CP exams.

Additionally, the conditions in your at-home or in-office environment will not likely match the controlled environment in which a SHRM-CP exam is administered. For these reasons, the practice items are intended to give a preview of the structure and format of test questions. It is not appropriate to use these results to predict an outcome on your exam, and doing well on the practice test is not a guarantee of a passing result on your exam.

Additional information, including the answer key and rationales for the correct answers for knowledge and foundational knowledge items, appear at the end of the practice test. Answer keys are also provided for the situational judgment items, but rationales are not provided due to the inherent nature of how these items are developed. Situational judgment items require judgment and decision-making to address workplace incidents, rather than relying on policy or law. All response options are actions that could be taken to respond to the situation, but there is only one *most effective* response. The most effective response is determined by diverse groups of experienced SHRM-certified HR professionals from around the globe who rate the effectiveness of each response. They also use the proficiency indicators outlined by the nine behavioral competencies in the SHRM BASK. Scoring of the most effective response is only done if the group of HR experts agree that this is the best response of all given alternatives.

When answering the SJI questions, do not base your response on an approach that is specific to your organization. Rather, use your understanding of HR best practice, which is documented in the SHRM BASK, to select your response.

To further enhance your preparation for the exam, consider the SHRM Learning System—which includes full-length SHRM-CP and SHRM-SCP practice (timed) exams full of previously used test items along with learning modules and over 2,700 practice items to help fill in your knowledge gaps. The SHRM Learning System is offered in a variety of formats—self-study and virtual or in-person seminars—and through partner universities that are authorized to teach the SHRM Learning System content.

SHRM-CP Practice Test Questions

Section 1: This section has sixteen knowledge items (KIs).

1. What performance review system rates employees from highest to lowest in order of their performance?

   A. Competency-based

   B. 360-degree feedback

   C. Forced distribution

   D. Ranking

2. What is the final step in Kotter's eight-step change model?

   A. Form a powerful coalition with organizational leaders.

   B. Communicate the vision to employees.

   C. Set future goals for continuous improvement.

   D. Anchor the change in the organization.

3. An HR director contacts department heads to collect data on internal and external factors that affect their staffing needs, current activity levels, and projected workloads. What step in workforce planning is the manager completing?

    A. Demand forecasting

    B. Gap analysis

    C. Supply forecasting

    D. Turnover analysis

4. A manager suspects an employee is under the influence of an illegal drug at work, which violates the company's drug-free workplace policy. The manager reports the incident to the HR manager. Which action should the HR manager take first?

    A. Meet with the employee's peers to confirm the manager's observations.

    B. Recommend the employee reach out to the company's employee assistance program.

    C. Give the employee a written warning and follow progressive discipline principles.

    D. Consult with legal counsel for advice about how to address the situation.

5. Which planning technique should an HR manager use to estimate the longest amount of time needed to complete essential tasks for a project?

    A. Variance analysis

    B. Gantt charts

    C. Critical path analysis

    D. Outcome monitoring

6. Which technique is most effective when giving a presentation to a diverse audience?

    A. Clearly read aloud and explain each bullet point in your presentation.

    B. Use appropriate non-verbal cues to help communicate your message.

    C. Ask audience members to save questions for the end of the presentation.

    D. Speak informally to be more relatable to the audience.

7. What system offers HR the capability to store employee records, provide online recruitment, extract metrics and reporting, and provide e-learning?

    A. Database management system

    B. HRIS

    C. Learning management system

    D. Applicant tracking system

8. Which action should an HR manager take to implement a newly developed corporate social responsibility and sustainability program?

    A.   Advise managers to develop and oversee programs for their respective departments.

    B.   Issue a memo to employees that outlines the program and expectations.

    C.   Work with stakeholders to implement a strategy across the organization.

    D.   Hire a consultant skilled in this area to lead the program and implementation.

9. Which advantage of instructor-led learning is lost in the transition from classroom to asynchronous online learning?

    A.   Opportunities to interact, ask questions, explore issues, and share ideas in real time.

    B.   Students can work in teams to help them work through problems and get feedback.

    C.   Different instructors can teach the same class and customize the content to meet specific needs.

    D.   In-person training is the most effective choice for presenting purely factual information and mechanical skills.

10. Which practice should an HR professional use to effectively manage the relationship with an outsourcing partner?

    A.   Create a formalized statement of expected benefits.

    B.   Track HR ratios and give feedback to management.

    C.   Use standardized vendor registration forms.

    D.   Solicit feedback on vendors from industry colleagues.

11. Which advice should an HR manager give to a part-time colleague who is facing constant job performance issues as a result of family and financial issues?

    A.   Request flextime to manage work and home.

    B.   Enroll in the employee assistance program.

    C.   Ask the company to remain on a part-time schedule.

    D.   Take training programs to enhance performance.

12. An employee is upset that the year-end bonus is not as much as expected. How should the HR manager address the employee's concerns while maintaining the employee's morale and current performance level?

    A.   Call the employee's department manager and have the manager respond to the employee's concerns.

    B.   Tell the employee that bonuses are not guaranteed and the employee should be thankful for what was received.

    C.   Listen to and empathize with the employee's concerns and then explain how the bonus program works.

    D.   Ask the employee for feedback on how the company could improve the current bonus program.

13. According to Tuckman's Ladder of Team Development, at which stage are teams most likely to pursue an ineffective solution to maintain positive relationships with peers?

    A. Forming

    B. Storming

    C. Norming

    D. Performing

14. An expatriate works for a foreign-based company in the expatriate's home country. Which type of work assignment is this considered?

    A. Host country national

    B. Third country resident

    C. Home country national

    D. Foreign service employee

15. What is the purpose of a job analysis?

    A. Inclusion and diversity

    B. Training and development

    C. Contractual modalities

    D. Risk analysis

16. Which method of dispute resolution should an HR VP recommend to quickly finalize a binding resolution?

    A. Arbitration

    B. Conciliation

    C. Ombudsman

    D. Step review

Section 2: This section has eighteen situational judgment items (SJIs).

The following scenario accompanies the next two items.

A small company hires a new HR manager to perform most HR roles in the company. Soon after the HR manager is hired, two employees resign. Both employees state they resigned because they believe there is an issue with the performance management system. They claim that employees are rewarded based on their relationships with their managers rather than actual performance. The HR manager decides to investigate the performance management system for potential areas of rater bias between managers.

The HR manager discovers that there is no formal structure to the performance management system. It utilizes a large annual review almost exclusively based on unstandardized supervisor ratings. Furthermore, the HR manager discovers disparities in pay and career progression between different employee groups, possibly resulting from the managers favoring employees who are similar to themselves. After summarizing the results to leadership, the new HR manager is tasked with updating the performance management system to account for potential rater bias and ultimately improve rating accuracy and equity. The HR manager drafts a new performance management system.

17. How should the HR manager assess the accuracy of the new performance management system before it is fully implemented?

    A. Benchmark the new system against similar companies in the same industry.

    B. Consult with leadership to ensure the draft aligns with overall organizational goals.

    C. Facilitate focus groups with employees to learn their views of the new system.

    D. Compile a companywide performance management report covering the past three years.

18. Which action should the HR manager take to investigate whether the company has inclusion and diversity (I&D) concerns in other areas of the company?

    A. Interview department managers about the I&D atmosphere of their departments.

    B. Launch an anonymous survey assessing employee opinions on I&D.

    C. Conduct focus groups to discuss employee experiences with I&D.

    D. Ask employees to provide testimonials about their I&D experiences at the company.

The following scenario accompanies the next three items.

An HR generalist working in a public healthcare facility is tasked with addressing the shortage of qualified job applicants for a specialized clinical position. Historically, the position has been difficult to fill because the few medical professionals who choose the specialty area tend to work for private sector organizations. In response, the facility's management decided to establish partnerships with two local post-secondary education institutions, a technical school and a public university, to develop training programs for the specialty area. Over the past few years, the facility has hired numerous graduates from both institutions.

Recently, graduates from the university have been showing significant technical performance deficiencies during the first several weeks on the job. Mistakes made by the graduates have been dangerous and costly for the facility. In addition, the technical school has been encouraging its graduates to seek employment in private organizations because salaries are typically higher. The healthcare facility's management no longer wants to hire applicants who graduated from the local institutions and is seeking advice on how to navigate the issues.

19. What incentive should the HR generalist recommend to the healthcare facility's management to encourage the institutions to improve their graduates' skills and motivate interest in working at the facility?

    A. Grant the institutions the opportunity to advertise as an approved educator for jobs with the facility.

    B. Create a specialized internship program exclusive to students at the two educational institutions.

    C. Guarantee job placement for graduates who meet a minimum grade point average and pass an entry-level screening exam.

    D. Publish a video advertisement that promotes the facility's benefits package and work environment.

20. What strategy should the HR generalist recommend to the healthcare facility's management to ensure the facility hires qualified candidates?

    A. Recruit and hire graduates from the technical school only.

    B. Develop a standard interviewing and hiring process for all managers to follow.

    C. Implement a cognitive ability assessment for all applicants.

    D. Require one manager to screen all applicants.

21. The HR professional is concerned that refusing to hire applicants who graduated from the local institutions will exclude more than 90% of their applicant population, including qualified graduates. What action should the HR professional take to persuade management to reconsider hiring graduates from local institutions?

A.   Perform a cost-benefit analysis to determine the impact of reduced staffing on patient care quality.

B.   Conduct a career and salary survey to identify options for restructuring the facility's compensation strategy.

C.   Compare the rates of hire for applicants from these institutions with applicants from all other sources.

D.   Compile patient satisfaction data to identify variance in care quality between graduates and non-graduates.

The following scenario accompanies the next two items.

After a merger of three companies, dissatisfied employees present the HR VP with competitor job posts displaying higher salaries for similar positions. Before the merger, managers at each company used non-standardized methods to determine salaries for their direct reports. This has resulted in varying levels of compensation for similar positions throughout the new company and frustrated employees because they do not understand how their pay is determined. This has led to an increasingly negative work environment with employees threatening to leave. The HR VP hires a consultant to work with the HR generalist to establish a new compensation package, which would compensate employees 25% above the market average for their positions. The new compensation package initiative is communicated to employees, including the target of 25% above the market average.

The consultant tells the HR generalist that to create a new compensation package with these goals, they must conduct a compensation study. The HR generalist knows the HR VP was hoping to avoid conducting a compensation study, but decides to move forward with the plan.

22. How should the HR generalist communicate the results of the compensation study to employees?

    A. Deliver a presentation at a company meeting to describe the methodology and results of the study.

    B. Ask the consultant to present at a company meeting to describe the methodology and results.

    C. Periodically send email updates to all employees on the study's progress to keep everyone informed.

    D. Provide a summary to managers and ask them to disseminate the information to their teams.

23. The HR VP tells the HR generalist that based on the results of the study, the company cannot afford to compensate employees at 25% above the market average. What should be the next course of action for the HR generalist?

    A. Offer to re-run the data without the high range to reduce the study's results.

    B. Meet with the HR VP to discuss alternative options and potential solutions.

    C. Investigate the possibility of reducing other benefits so the salary target can be reached.

    D. Suggest exploring early retirement incentives to allocate more money to the salary target.

The following scenario accompanies the next two items.

The HR manager at a grocery store is meeting with the store's general manager when the meeting is interrupted by two police officers. The officers inform the general and HR managers that one of the store's employees was in a fatal car accident while driving to work. The employee was a relatively new, part-time employee who was well-liked by management and staff. The police officers request the contact information of the employee's emergency contact, and then they leave the store. No other employees are informed of the situation by the officers, but many notice the officers' presence and become concerned that something is wrong. The general manager wants to respond appropriately to the difficult situation but would like to minimize the disruption to store operations.

24. After learning about the accident, several employees request time off from work while they grieve. The general manager is concerned that there may not be enough employees to adequately staff the store and asks for the HR manager's advice. What should the HR manager recommend?

    A. Grant all requests for unpaid time off and invite other employees to work overtime to cover gaps.

    B. Offer time off to any employee who requests it, but limit the amount of time off that can be requested.

    C. Grant requests only to those employees who worked closely with the deceased employee.

    D. Provide unpaid time off to employees to attend the employee's funeral service only.

25. A few weeks after the accident, one of the employee's co-workers complains to the HR manager that the store's management team cares more about the financial interests of the company than the employees' well-being. How should the HR manager respond?

    A. Relay the concern to the store's general manager, but keep the co-worker's identity confidential.

    B. Ask other employees at the store if they believe the management team has acted insensitively.

    C. Explain that the leadership team has tried to consider the staff's emotional needs during the difficult time.

    D. Invite the co-worker to a private meeting to discuss the concerns in more detail.

The following scenario accompanies the next three items.

The board of trustees of a well-known college is concerned that the current pay policies are not sustainable. Several of the highest paid employees are classroom instructors who earn more than the vice presidents. Because all pay authorizations are the responsibility of the HR department, the board authorizes the HR department manager to investigate the college's pay policies and procedures. The HR manager begins conducting an audit of the college's payroll records and discovers that bonuses are being offered to some employees without documentation of their merit or achievement, in violation of the college's merit-based bonus policy.

Additionally, some instructors are receiving extra pay for special programs they conduct during their normal work hours, and one instructor is being paid for three classes running concurrently in the same room. The HR manager also learns that the individual who is supposed to manage the payroll department only has authority to process payroll transactions. As a result, no one has analyzed trends and exceptions that need to be addressed by the president and the board.

26. The HR manager wants to invite college employees to a focus group to develop a change management strategy for correcting the payment policies and practices. What is the most effective approach the manager should take to ensure the participation of individuals who will be affected by the new policy?

    A.   Offer to meet with each person individually to answer their questions.

    B.   Conduct outreach presentations with each department to generate enthusiasm.

    C.   Send an email to all employees to solicit volunteer participation.

    D.   Ask the board to approve an incentive for participation.

27. The HR manager finds numerous transfer requests from employees wishing to transfer to a department that routinely offers bonuses to all staff members regardless of their performance quality. What should the HR manager do to ensure that managers understand that bonuses must be tied to specific work-related behaviors?

    A.   Revise the bonus-approval policy to prevent the authorization of bonuses that are not merit-based.

    B.   Send out communication in the staff newsletter highlighting the bonus policy for all employees.

    C.   Remind the managers of potential negative implications of bonuses that are not tied to performance.

    D.   Conduct a training for all managers to reinforce the college's merit-based bonus policy.

28. During the exchange of several emails between the HR department and the board regarding the progress of the audit, one of the board members copies the college's football coach. What should the HR manager do to ensure unauthorized individuals do not receive emails about the audit?

   A. Notify the board member privately that information related to the audit must not be shared with other college employees.

   B. Send an email to all HR staff reminding them about the importance of confidentiality regarding the audit.

   C. Require the board member and college's football coach to sign a non-disclosure agreement.

   D. Advise the board that no additional information related to the audit will be provided until the board identifies a solution to protect sensitive information.

The following scenario accompanies the next two items.

The HR director meets with the CEO to discuss concerns about the lack of accessibility for people with disabilities. The company completed an employee engagement survey two calendar years ago. The data revealed that the employees are disappointed in the company's slow action in taking steps to make improvements in the workplace for people with disabilities. Most recently, data from customer feedback also show that customers with disabilities found it much harder to resolve an issue than customers without disabilities. After an organizational restructure, the executive team decides that the current HRIS needs to be re-evaluated to determine if the system still meets the needs of the business and HR customers.

The HR team sees this as an excellent opportunity to kick-start the company's accessibility initiative. The HR team is responsible for making this decision and is given the authority to make the change to a new system. However, one executive team member expresses displeasure with allowing the HR team to have this authority. The contract renewal date for the current HRIS is approaching soon, so a decision to keep it or transfer to a new system needs to be quickly made.

29. The HR manager identifies several potential HRIS options. Which approach should the HR manager take to determine the best HRIS for the company?

    A.   Present each option to the HR team for their feedback.

    B.   Choose the HRIS that will address the most challenges.

    C.   Conduct a cost-benefit analysis for each HRIS option.

    D.   Use a survey to gather feedback from all employees.

30. An executive team member suggests a particular HRIS vendor to the HR manager. The HR manager later learns that this member has investments in the vendor. The vendor's HRIS is more expensive than competing products but would address organizational needs. How should the HR manager address the conflict of interest?

    A.   Tell the members of the executive team about the conflict of interest.

    B.   Remove the HRIS vendor from the list of vendors being considered.

    C.   Recommend the executive team member sell the investments in the vendor.

    D.   Obtain an opinion from the legal department about the conflict of interest.

The following scenario accompanies the next two items.

The CEO of a midsize company with several regional offices authorizes an employee climate survey. The survey used to be conducted annually, but due to turnover in the HR department, it has not been conducted in five years. The CEO appoints the HR generalist to lead the survey and asks for a team representative from each department. The new team designs the survey for companywide distribution, and the results reveal both strengths and areas for improvement. While employees are optimistic about company growth and new hires, employees are concerned that those with different backgrounds are marginalized.

Survey data also shows employees are frustrated by the lack of career growth and chances for leadership opportunities. Finally, the data indicates employees are dissatisfied with their work–life balance because employees are expected to work full time in the office. The HR generalist meets with the CEO and recommends that the survey team remain together to address the top three issues affecting the company, which include increasing inclusion and diversity, providing more training opportunities, and offering more flexible work options. The CEO agrees and approves the team for the next twelve months.

31. Several employees indicate they must use personal time for religious observations and do not feel their celebrations are treated equally. The HR generalist wants to institute a policy that honors all cultural and religious practices and resolves concerns about using personal time. Which should the HR generalist recommend?

    A. Institute a set number of floating holidays employees can use for religious or cultural celebrations.

    B. Incorporate virtual monthly celebrations highlighting all cultures to foster inclusion.

    C. Provide the option for employees to take small breaks during the workday for religious observations.

    D. Organize a companywide, diversity-themed event for employees to bring items that represent their cultural heritage.

32. The CEO prefers employees to be in the office and does not support remote work. However, many managers allow team members to work from home, which angers the CEO. How can the HR generalist highlight the benefits of remote work for the CEO?

    A. Present data that remote work can result in reduced turnover rates and cost savings.

    B. Show that the company can grow without having to add more office space since employees work from home.

    C. Explain that allowing employees the freedom to work remotely can increase morale.

    D. Mention that remote working reduces the opportunity for interpersonal conflicts between employees on site.

The following scenario accompanies the next two items.

An executive of a multinational company discloses participation in an intimate relationship with one of the company's managers to the HR manager. The relationship has been ongoing for several months, and both parties confirm with HR that the relationship is consensual. The company has a policy about office relationships between peers and advises against relationships between employees and their direct supervisors, but the policy does not directly prohibit such relationships. The manager is scheduled for a promotion that would put the executive in a direct supervisory role over the manager. Additionally, several recent incidents involving the executive and manager may be perceived as favoritism. The HR manager needs to address the relationship to mitigate risks to the company and employees due to potential perceptions of favoritism.

33. The HR manager recommends updating the policy to clarify the rules regarding intimate relationships between executives and direct reports. Which approach should the HR manager take to demonstrate to the leadership team why this update is necessary?

    A. Describe how relationships between individuals in supervisory roles increases the company's exposure to conflicts of interest.

    B. Explain the potential for perceived favoritism and the resulting employee resentment and mistrust.

    C. Frame the update as a way to ensure fair treatment for all employees involved in intimate relationships with other employees at the company.

    D. Show how the policy can streamline HR processes and minimize disruptions to future succession planning.

34. The executive approved a telework request for the manager prior to the relationship disclosure. Another long-term employee approaches the executive with a similar request and is denied. The employee complains to the HR manager about being denied. Which action should the HR manager take to mitigate perceptions of favoritism regarding telework agreements?

    A. Suggest the executive withdraw the manager's telework approval to minimize the appearance of bias.

    B. Develop a standardized process for telework requests and criteria for approval of the requests.

    C. Approve the long-term employee's request since the manager's request was previously approved.

    D. Review company job descriptions to determine if telework is a viable option for the long-term employee.

Section 3: This section has sixteen knowledge items (KIs).

35. An employer discovers many of its employees do not feel their work has meaning or purpose. Which action best addresses the root cause of this issue?

    A. Identify measurable steps to develop a culture of recognition.

    B. Launch a job shadowing program for employees to explore other functions.

    C. Develop a bonus incentive program to motivate employees to work harder.

    D. Organize a series of workplace team-building efforts to encourage cohesiveness.

36. When developing a business case, which strategy minimizes problems or issues during implementation?

    A. Limit financial metrics to industry benchmarks.

    B. Propose various courses of action.

    C. Incorporate qualitative feedback from leadership.

    D. Be specific and clear about the problem.

37. Which is a primary benefit of integrating artificial intelligence into routine HR candidate-screening practices?

    A. Provides career development tips to prospective candidates.

    B. Identifies top-quality candidates objectively while removing selection bias.

    C. Tracks common candidate questions then generates automatic responses.

    D. Implements new algorithms to hire candidates based on less information about candidates.

38. An employee earns $5,000 less than a colleague of the opposite sex who has the same responsibilities and a similar background. The employee last received a paycheck 60 days ago. Under what law does the employee have the right to file a discrimination claim?

    A. Fair Labor Standards Act of 1938

    B. National Labor Relations Act of 1947

    C. Equal Pay Act of 1963

    D. Lily Ledbetter Fair Pay Act of 2009

39. What is the purpose of a work breakdown structure?

    A. Identify the components of a project

    B. Develop a detailed schedule for a project

    C. Outline the technical details of a project

    D. Create a budget for a project

40. A reduction in force strategy is needed at a struggling startup. All employees are full time and most have worked for the company for a similar amount of time. Which strategy should be used to determine which staff are laid off?

    A. Skills

    B. Seniority

    C. Merit

    D. Employee status

41. A company is expanding globally for the first time and needs an employee for an international assignment. What is the most important factor the company should consider before selecting an employee for the opportunity?

    A. Salary

    B. Environmental conditions

    C. A successor for the current position

    D. Family readiness

42. Engagement survey results indicate that most employees enjoy their jobs but do not believe their skills and abilities are being fully utilized. Which method of job design should be implemented to most improve team engagement?

    A. Job simplification

    B. Job enrichment

    C. Job enlargement

    D. Job rotation

43. Which recommendation should an HR business partner make to the leadership team of a midsize insurance company on the best way to restructure the organization while keeping administrative costs low?

    A. Divide employees into two departments by the primary product they support.

    B. Group employees by the customer type they interact with the most.

    C. Organize employees by their respective function.

    D. Create departments based on employees' locations.

44. Which step should an HR manager take after conducting a job analysis using the point method?

    A. Identify the compensable factors.

    B. Document the required knowledge.

    C. Measure internal equity across the team.

    D. Determine whether the job is a benchmark job.

45. How can HR best support an organization's transition from in-person teams to hybrid teams?

    A. Conduct a survey to determine employees' working preferences.

    B. Create a written policy that clearly defines the expectations.

    C. Provide additional resources to employees working from home.

    D. Increase the budget to cover cost of IT equipment.

46. Which is the primary outcome of using mediation in the conflict resolution process?

    A. Imposing a settlement by a neutral third party

    B. Reaching a mutual agreement between two parties

    C. Issuing a non-binding settlement

    D. Establishing a confidentiality agreement

47. Which situation poses a potential workplace conflict of interest?

    A. Two entry-level employees meet for dinner after work to discuss a workplace rumor.

    B. An IT system analyst establishes a company for IT consultation services after retirement.

    C. An employee provides consulting services for a company in which the employee's relative processes payroll.

    D. An employee working in the HR department issues the monthly timesheet record for thier spouse.

48. What is the first step in developing an effective recruitment process?

    A. Develop a recruitment strategy.

    B. Prioritize recruitment activities.

    C. Establish recruitment objectives.

    D. Identify recruitment metrics.

49. Which action should the HR manager take to most effectively ensure the long-term retention of institutional knowledge at an organization with many employees planning to retire in the near future?

    A. Engage managers at every level in the implementation of succession planning programs.

    B. Encourage the potential retirees to transfer their tacit knowledge to their less experienced peers.

    C. Conduct multigenerational training sessions to smooth the transition between generations.

    D. Offer an employment extension to these employees to retain their experience.

50. Which performance assessment method lists several job dimensions and a range of performance values for a trait or behavior?

    A.   Graphic rating scale

    B.   Alternation ranking

    C.   Paired comparison

    D.   Forced distribution

Appendix 1

The SHRM-CP Practice Test Answers

Question Number	Item Data		Rationale
1	Domain	People	"Ranking" is correct because this method lists all employees in a designated group from highest to lowest in order of performance.
	Sub-Competency	Employee Engagement & Retention	
	Difficulty	Easy	
	Key	D	
2	Domain	Business	"Anchor the change in the organization." is correct because according to John Kotter's Eight-Step Change Model, the final stem is to make change stick, reinforce the value of the successful change, and make sure relevant policies, procedures and practices are being followed.
	Sub-Competency	Consultation	
	Difficulty	Hard	
	Key	D	
3	Domain	Organization	"Demand forecasting" is correct because demand forecasts are based on data relating to forecast activity levels and the implications of business and operational plans, together with information from scenario planning.
	Sub-Competency	Workforce Management	
	Difficulty	Somewhat Hard	
	Key	A	
4	Domain	Workplace	"Consult with legal counsel for advice about how to address the situation." is the correct answer because regardless of whether the manager's suspicions are correct, it is important to protect the company by getting legal advice before investigating and addressing the issue with the employee.
	Sub-Competency	Risk Management	
	Difficulty	Somewhat Hard	
	Key	D	
5	Domain	People	"Critical path analysis" is correct because it specifically calculates the longest path of all essential activities to logical end points or to the end of the project.
	Sub-Competency	HR Strategy	
	Difficulty	Hard	
	Key	C	

6	Domain	Interpersonal	"Use appropriate non-verbal cues to help communicate your message" is correct because nonverbal cues, such as posture, gestures, and tone of voice, have the power to support or detract from your intended message. For example, crossed arms is seen as a closed-off posture and would not be appropriate for a discussion on open communication; in this instance it would be best to adopt a relaxed stance and a welcoming tone of voice. It is also important to note that some common gestures may be offensive to other cultures.
	Sub-Competency	Communication	
	Difficulty	Somewhat Hard	
	Key	B	
7	Domain	Organization	"HRIS" is correct because it performs several functions including storing employee records, providing online recruitment, pulling metrics and reporting, and providing e-learning. The other answers only provide one of those capabilities, not all.
	Sub-Competency	Technology Management	
	Difficulty	Easy	
	Key	B	
8	Domain	Workplace	"Work with stakeholders to implement a strategy across the organization" is correct because HR must carry out this initiative and not pass it off to a consultant or department managers. Although hiring a consultant could be a viable second option, if the HR manager is not skilled in this area. Simply issuing a memo to employees is not an effective method of implementing the program.
	Sub-Competency	Corporate Social Responsibility	
	Difficulty	Easy	
	Key	C	
9	Domain	People	"Opportunities to interact, ask questions, explore issues, and share ideas in real-time" is correct because they learn from one another as well as from the instructor.
	Sub-Competency	Learning & Development	
	Difficulty	Somewhat Easy	
	Key	A	
10	Domain	Organization	"Create a formalized statement of expected benefits" is correct because the key to successful outsourcing of HR functions is to successfully manage relationships with outsourcing partners, which involves establishing a collaborative way of working with vendors to establish trust and open communication. This can be accomplished by creating a formalized statement of expected benefits that includes quantitative and qualitative targets and by using established practices that have demonstrated good outcomes.
	Sub-Competency	Structure of the HR Function	
	Difficulty	Somewhat Easy	
	Key	A	
11	Domain	People	"Enroll in Employee Assistance Program" is correct because this is an educational treatment focused on employee psychological wellbeing and works around how to manage difficult situations in personal life.
	Sub-Competency	Total Rewards	
	Difficulty	Somewhat Easy	
	Key	B	

12	Domain	Leadership	"Listen to and empathize with the employee's concerns and then explain how the bonus program works" is correct because the HR manager should listen to and empathize with employees to validate their feelings and then share how programs work so the employee has a better understanding for the future.
	Sub-Competency	Leadership & Navigation	
	Difficulty	Easy	
	Key	C	
13	Domain	Organization	"Norming" is correct because according to Tuckman's Ladder of Team Development, this is the stage at which the group is most likely to avoid conflict in order to maintain harmony. A key indicator of the forming stage would be lack of communication, storming would be conflict, and performing would be role development and fluidity.
	Sub-Competency	Organizational Effectiveness & Development	
	Difficulty	Hard	
	Key	C	
14	Domain	Workplace	"Host country national" is correct because this term is used for the expatriate who is working in their home country but for the foreign company.
	Sub-Competency	Managing a Global Workforce	
	Difficulty	Hard	
	Key	A	
15	Domain	People	"Training and development" is correct answer because before identifying the information required for job analysis, an analyst should be clear about the purpose of job analysis. Job analysis can have single or multiple purpose. Only HR training and development is relevant; all other options are out of scope.
	Sub-Competency	Talent Acquisition	
	Difficulty	Easy	
	Key	B	
16	Domain	Organization	"Arbitration" is correct because an arbitrator is a neutral third party who imposes a final, binding decision to resolve a dispute. Because the parties cannot come to an agreement, arbitration is the best option.
	Sub-Competency	Employee & Labor Relations	
	Difficulty	Somewhat Easy	
	Key	A	
17	Domain	Business	Situational judgment items (SJIs) require the examinee to think about what is occurring in the scenario and decide which response option identifies the most effective course of action. Other response options may be something you *could* do to respond in the situation, but SJIs require thinking and acting based on the best of the available options. Do not base your answer on your organization's approach to handling the situation; rather, answer based on what you know *should* be done according to best practice. Panels of SHRM-certified subject matter experts rate the effectiveness of each response option, and the *best* answer is derived by statistical analysis of those expert opinions.
	Sub-Competency	Business Acumen	
	Difficulty	Somewhat Hard	
	Key	B	
18	Domain	Leadership	
	Sub-Competency	Inclusion & Diversity	
	Difficulty	Somewhat Easy	
	Key	B	

19	Domain	Interpersonal	
	Sub-Competency	Relationship Management	
	Difficulty	Somewhat Easy	
	Key	B	
20	Domain	Business	
	Sub-Competency	Business Acumen	
	Difficulty	Somewhat Hard	
	Key	B	
21	Domain	Business	
	Sub-Competency	Business Acumen	
	Difficulty	Somewhat Hard	
	Key	C	
22	Domain	Interpersonal	
	Sub-Competency	Communication	
	Difficulty	Somewhat Hard	
	Key	C	
23	Domain	Leadership	
	Sub-Competency	Ethical Practice	
	Difficulty	Easy	
	Key	B	
24	Domain	Business	
	Sub-Competency	Consultation	
	Difficulty	Hard	
	Key	A	
25	Domain	Interpersonal	
	Sub-Competency	Communication	
	Difficulty	Somewhat Easy	
	Key	D	
26	Domain	Interpersonal	
	Sub-Competency	Relationship Management	
	Difficulty	Somewhat Hard	
	Key	A	

Situational judgment items (SJIs) require the examinee to think about what is occurring in the scenario and decide which response option identifies the most effective course of action. Other response options may be something you *could* do to respond in the situation, but SJIs require thinking and acting based on the best of the available options. Do not base your answer on your organization's approach to handling the situation; rather, answer based on what you know *should* be done according to best practice. Panels of SHRM-certified subject matter experts rate the effectiveness of each response option, and the *best* answer is derived by statistical analysis of those expert opinions.

27	Domain	Interpersonal
	Sub-Competency	Commincation
	Difficulty	Somewhat Easy
	Key	D
28	Domain	Leadership
	Sub-Competency	Ethical Practice
	Difficulty	Somewhat Hard
	Key	A
29	Domain	Business
	Sub-Competency	Analytical Aptitude
	Difficulty	Somewhat Hard
	Key	C
30	Domain	Leadership
	Sub-Competency	Ethical Practice
	Difficulty	Somewhat Easy
	Key	D
31	Domain	Interpersonal
	Sub-Competency	Global Mindset
	Difficulty	Easy
	Key	A
32	Domain	Business
	Sub-Competency	Business Acumen
	Difficulty	Somewhat Hard
	Key	A
33	Domain	Business
	Sub-Competency	Consultation
	Difficulty	Hard
	Key	A
34	Domain	Leadership
	Sub-Competency	Ethical Practice
	Difficulty	Easy
	Key	B

Situational judgment items (SJIs) require the examinee to think about what is occurring in the scenario and decide which response option identifies the most effective course of action. Other response options may be something you *could* do to respond in the situation, but SJIs require thinking and acting based on the best of the available options. Do not base your answer on your organization's approach to handling the situation; rather, answer based on what you know *should* be done according to best practice. Panels of SHRM-certified subject matter experts rate the effectiveness of each response option, and the *best* answer is derived by statistical analysis of those expert opinions.

35	Domain	People	"Identify measurable steps to develop a culture of recognition" is correct because recognition is directly connected with employee job satisfaction.
	Sub-Competency	Employee Engagement & Retention	
	Difficulty	Somewhat Easy	
	Key	A	
36	Domain	Business	"Be specific and clear about the problem" is correct because the problem statement should be one paragraph or less and list the specific business problem. A common problem is when the business problem is poorly identified or stated.
	Sub-Competency	Business Acumen	
	Difficulty	Somewhat Hard	
	Key	D	
37	Domain	Organization	"Provides career development tips to prospective candidates" is correct because artificial intelligence technology can match candidates to a position with a high degree of accuracy without succumbing.
	Sub-Competency	Technology Management	
	Difficulty	Easy	
	Key	B	
38	Domain	Workplace	"Lily Ledbetter Fair Pay Act of 2009" is correct because this act said that each paycheck that delivers discriminatory compensation is actionable under the federal Equal Employment Opportunity statutes, regardless of when the discrimination began. Under the act, an individual can file a charge within 180 days (or 300 days depending upon the jurisdiction) of any paycheck that is based on a discriminatory decision.
	Sub-Competency	U.S. Employment Law & Regulations	
	Difficulty	Somewhat Hard	
	Key	D	
39	Domain	People	"Identify the components of a project" is correct because a work breakdown structure (WBS) is defined as "a hierarchical decomposition of the total scope of work to be carried out by the project team to accomplish the project objectives and create the required deliverables." A WBS does not include a schedule or budget for a project. The WBS includes technical details of a project but they are not the sole focus of a WBS.
	Sub-Competency	HR Strategy	
	Difficulty	Somewhat Easy	
	Sub-Competency	A	
40	Domain	Organization	"Skills" is correct because a skills-based reduction in force selection process is most appropriate. The CFO should work with other leadership managers (including HR if there is a dedicated HR person) to determine which skill sets are most essential.
	Sub-Competency	Workforce Management	
	Difficulty	Somewhat Easy	
	Key	A	

41	Domain	Workplace	"Family readiness" is correct because ensuring the transition is smooth for the employee's family with contribute to their overall well-being and success on the assignment.
	Sub-Competency	Managing a Global Workforce	
	Difficulty	Hard	
	Key	D	
42	Domain	People	"Job enrichment" is correct because it would increase meaningfulness and variety of the work.
	Sub-Competency	Employee Engagement & Retention	
	Difficulty	Somewhat Hard	
	Key	B	
43	Domain	Organization	"Organize employees by their respective function" is correct because this is an example of a functional design structure, which is best for smaller companies and keeps administrative costs low.
	Sub-Competency	Organizational Effectiveness & Development	
	Difficulty	Somewhat Easy	
	Key	C	
44	Domain	People	"Identify compensable factors" is correct because each compensable factor must be evaluated on organizational value.
	Sub-Competency	Total Rewards	
	Difficulty	Somewhat Hard	
	Key	A	
45	Domain	Workplace	"Create a written policy that clearly defines the expectations" is correct because employees must have access to a clearly written policy that defines the expectations of how the hybrid-approach will apply based on different criteria. This will allow for greater alignment and ensure equity and transparency in the process.
	Sub-Competency	Managing a Global Workforce	
	Difficulty	Somewhat Easy	
	Key	B	
46	Domain	Organization	"Reaching a mutual agreement between two parties" is correct because the goal of the mediator is to help the negotiator avoid or resolve and impasses by reaching a decision.
	Sub-Competency	Employee & Labor Relations	
	Difficulty	Easy	
	Key	B	
47	Domain	Leadership	"An employee working in the HR department issues the monthly timesheet record for their spouse" is correct because the personal relationship between the two employees could compromise their judgment within the workplace.
	Sub-Competency	Ethical Practice	
	Difficulty	Somewhat Easy	
	Key	D	

48	Domain	People	"Establish recruitment objectives" is correct because according to the SHRM model of the Employee Recruitment Process, the first step in the recruitment process should be establishing objectives which sets the parameters for the ensuing steps of the process: strategy development, recruitment activities and results evaluation.
	Sub-Competency	Talent Acquisition	
	Difficulty	Somewhat Easy	
	Key	C	
49	Domain	Organization	"Engage managers at every level in the implementation of the succession planning programs" is correct because with succession planning, knowledge transfer can occur concurrently between the baby boomers and the potential successor, giving the successor the unique opportunity to gain useful skills and knowledge. It is the role of managers to identify successors and engage in the learning process.
	Sub-Competency	Workforce Management	
	Difficulty	Somewhat Easy	
	Key	A	
50	Domain	Business	"Graphic rating scale" is correct because this is the simplest and most popular method for appraising performance. The supervisor rates the performance of the employee by indicating the appropriate level of performance from low to high performance. This scale provides assessment to an objective metric rather than another person.
	Sub-Competency	Analytical Aptitude	
	Difficulty	Somewhat Hard	
	Key	A	

Appendix 2

Twelve-Week Study Schedule Template

We have provided a set of study schedule templates to guide your SHRM-CP exam preparation. Please use these spaces to create your plan and write it down.

Planned Test Date with Prometric: _____

Study Week 1: _____

Weekly Goal: This week, I will...

_____

_____

_____

_____

	Planned Time	Study Focus
Sunday		
Monday		
Tuesday		
Wednesday		
Thursday		
Friday		
Saturday		

Study Week 2: _____

Weekly Goal: This week, I will...

_____

_____

_____

_____

	Planned Time	Study Focus
Sunday		
Monday		
Tuesday		
Wednesday		
Thursday		
Friday		
Saturday		

Study Week 3: _____

Weekly Goal: This week, I will...

_____

_____

_____

_____

	Planned Time	Study Focus
Sunday		
Monday		
Tuesday		
Wednesday		
Thursday		
Friday		
Saturday		

Study Week 4: _____

Weekly Goal: This week, I will...

_____

_____

_____

_____

	Planned Time	Study Focus
Sunday		
Monday		
Tuesday		
Wednesday		
Thursday		
Friday		
Saturday		

Study Week 5: _____

Weekly Goal: This week, I will...

_____

_____

_____

_____

	Planned Time	Study Focus
Sunday		
Monday		
Tuesday		
Wednesday		
Thursday		
Friday		
Saturday		

Study Week 6: _____

Weekly Goal: This week, I will...

_____

_____

_____

_____

	Planned Time	Study Focus
Sunday		
Monday		
Tuesday		
Wednesday		
Thursday		
Friday		
Saturday		

Study Week 7: _____

Weekly Goal: This week, I will...

_____

_____

_____

_____

	Planned Time	Study Focus
Sunday		
Monday		
Tuesday		
Wednesday		
Thursday		
Friday		
Saturday		

Study Week 8: _____

Weekly Goal: This week, I will...

_____

_____

_____

_____

	Planned Time	Study Focus
Sunday		
Monday		
Tuesday		
Wednesday		
Thursday		
Friday		
Saturday		

Study Week 9: _____

Weekly Goal: This week, I will...

_____

_____

_____

_____

	Planned Time	Study Focus
Sunday		
Monday		
Tuesday		
Wednesday		
Thursday		
Friday		
Saturday		

Study Week 10: _____

Weekly Goal: This week, I will...

_____

_____

_____

_____

	Planned Time	Study Focus
Sunday		
Monday		
Tuesday		
Wednesday		
Thursday		
Friday		
Saturday		

Study Week 11: _____

Weekly Goal: This week, I will...

_____

_____

_____

_____

	Planned Time	Study Focus
Sunday		
Monday		
Tuesday		
Wednesday		
Thursday		
Friday		
Saturday		

Study Week 12: _____

Weekly Goal: This week, I will...

_____

_____

_____

_____

	Planned Time	Study Focus
Sunday		
Monday		
Tuesday		
Wednesday		
Thursday		
Friday		
Saturday		

About SHRM Books

SHRM Books develops and publishes insights, ideas, strategies, and solutions on the topics that matter most to human resource professionals, people managers, and students.

The strength of our program lies in the expertise and thought leadership of our authors to educate, empower, elevate, and inspire readers around the world.

Each year, SHRM Books publishes new titles covering contemporary human resource management issues, as well as general workplace topics. With more than one hundred titles available in print, digital, and audio formats, SHRM's books can be purchased through SHRMStore.org and a variety of book retailers.

Learn more at SHRMBooks.org.

Index